(RE)ARTICULATING WRITING ASSESSMENT FOR TEACHING AND LEARNING

(RE)ARTICULATING WRITING ASSESSMENT FOR TEACHING AND LEARNING

BRIAN HUOT

UTAH STATE UNIVERSITY PRESS
Logan, Utah

Copyright © 2002 Utah State University Press
Logan, Utah 84322–7800
All rights reserved.
Manufactured in the United States of America.

Cover design by Sans Serif Inc.

A version of chapter three appeared in *College English* Vol 64, copyright © 2002 by the
National Council of Teachers of English. Reprinted with permission.

An early version of chapter four appeared in *College Composition and Communication*, Vol 47,
copyright © 1996 by the National Council of Teachers of English. Reprinted with permission.

Library of Congress Cataloging-in-Publication Data
Huot, Brian A.
  (Re)articulating writing assessment for teaching and learning / Brian Huot.
    p. cm.
Includes bibliographical references (p.) and index.
  ISBN 0-87421-449-1 (alk. paper)
 1. English language—Rhetoric—Study and teaching. 2. Grading and
marking (Students) 3. Report writing—Evaluation. 4. College
prose—Evaluation. I. Title.
  PE1404 .H86 2002
  808'.042'071—dc21
      2002010352

For Pam and Pat,
*without whom many of the good things in my life
(like this book) would not be possible.*

CONTENTS

ACKNOWLEDGMENTS

When I was in graduate school in the mid 1980s, Michael M. Williamson told me and my graduate student colleagues that no one did research alone. Over the years, I have come to realize just how accurate he was. I am dependent upon so many people for many of the ideas, insights and expressions in this book, that there is no way I could acknowledge everyone's contributions. I would like to start by thanking all of those people whose names do not appear in this acknowledgement. My omissions are due to the vast intellectual debts I owe for this book and my own inability to remember all of the help I have received.

There is no way I could have done the work I have during my professional life and in this book had not many scholars paved the way in writing assessment.

Among the many shoulders upon which I stand, I must mention Hunter Breland, Roberta Camp, Charles Cooper, Peter Elbow, Lester Faigley, Lee Odell and Stephen Witte. Of course, like anyone working in college writing assessment I am greatly indebted to Edward M. White for his trail blazing work over the last three or more decades. Although I have carefully documented the published sources I've used, the published work of some people has shaped this volume and helped me to create a text that would not be possible without their contributions. In this category, I would like to thank Arnetha Ball, Pat Belanoff, Harold Berlak, Roberta Camp, Lee Cronbach, Peter Elbow, Lester Faigley, Richard Haswell, George Madhaus, Samuel Messick, Pamela Moss, Sandra Murphy, Louise Phelps, Lorrie Shephard, William L. Smith, Melanie Sperling, Richard Straub,

Edward M. White, Michael M. Williamson, Kathleen Blake Yancey and James Zebroski. During the many years I took to write this text I have engaged in a wealth of conversations that have enhanced and increased my understanding. Among the many people who helped me talk through the issues and ideas that comprise this text, I thank Barry Alford, Bob Broad, Pat Carini, Vicki Hester, Joseph McCarren, Sandra Murphy, Michael Neal, Peggy O'Neill, Ellen Schendel, Jerry Schnick and Pamela Takayoshi. I would especially like to thank Michael M. Williamson for starting and sustaining a continuing, two-decade old conversation with me about writing assessment. I thank Bob Broad and Susanmarie Harrington for their detailed and insightful review of the book that helped me make many needed revisions. I would also like to thank Mary Fowles and Hunter Breland for providing me with references. I thank Linda Baldwin for her help in preparing the bibliography for the volume. Finally, I thank Pamela Takayoshi who read several early drafts of much of this text and without whom I might still be struggling to tame my words.

1

(RE)ARTICULATING WRITING ASSESSMENT

Naming this book has been quite an adventure. When the idea for its title and shape first came to mind, I originally thought to call it *Reclaiming Assessment for the Teaching of Writing*. Of course, as I thought through the title and reexamined the idea, I realized that to *re*claim something meant that it had to be claimed in the first place. Unfortunately, writing assessment has never been claimed as a part of the teaching of writing. As far back as 1840, writing assessment was hailed as a better technology (chapter six contains a discussion of writing assessment as technology) for assessing student knowledge (Witte, Trashel, and Walters 1986). The use of essay placement exams at Harvard and other prestigious institutions in the nineteenth century was justified in response to the growing perception that students were underprepared for the rigors of university study. This notion of assessment as something done because of a deficit in student training or teacher responsibility is still with us in the plethora of accountability programs at the state level for public schools and in the recent national assessment programs advocated by the George W. Bush administration and adopted by Congress. Throughout the twentieth century, writing assessment became the tool of administrators and politicians who wished to maintain an efficient and accountable educational bureaucracy (Williamson 1994). The literature about classroom assessment was limited to an irregular series of volumes on grading student writing (see Judine 1965, for an example). At any rate, it would be inaccurate for me to advocate the re-claiming of writing assessment, when in fact it has yet to be claimed for the teaching of writing.

RE-IMAGINING ASSESSMENT

Although I contend that writing assessment has yet to be claimed for teaching writing, I have also come to challenge the whole notion of claiming assessment at all. Probably my dissatisfaction comes from the association of claiming with the concept of the stakeholder, a concept I discuss in more detail in chapters two and seven. Although I recognize that assessment must be a multi-disciplinary enterprise, something that should never be driven completely by the beliefs and assumptions of any single group, I don't believe that all stakeholders should have equal claim, since those closest to teaching and learning, like students and teachers, need to have the most input about writing assessment and all important teaching decisions. If assessment is to be used as a positive force in the teaching of writing, then it makes sense that those with the most knowledge and training be those who make the most important decisions about student assessment. Using writing assessment to promote teaching is one of the most crucial messages in this book.

Once I rejected the idea of reclaiming assessment, for awhile I renamed the volume *Re-Imagining Assessment for the Teaching of Writing*, because I now realized that the assessment of writing had never been central to its teaching and that claiming was a problematic term for many reasons. Because this volume is an ambitious work that clearly extends beyond simply staking out a claim for teachers to assessment, I thought the idea of re-imagining would work because it seemed grander, bigger, more in keeping with the ambitious nature of my purpose. As I began to work on the volume, however, "re-imagine" seemed too grand, too big, too abstract. And, of course one could argue that we had never imagined assessment for the teaching of writing. In a response to an earlier, shorter version of chapter four published in *College Composition and Communication*, Alan Purves (1996) had objected to my use of the term "theory," as being too big and abstract since he thought what I had constructed was something practical, important and useful, but not theoretical. My concern with theory is that it can be construed as distinct from practice, and my intent in this book is to blur rather than emphasize any distinctions between theory and practice. As I detail in chapter seven, I was flattered by what he had to say, even if I didn't completely agree with him. On the other hand, I decided "re-imagine" was too big, since what I propose throughout this volume is less grand and more a reasoned response to the pressures, pitfalls and potential benefits from the assessment of student writing. My ideas that writing assessment can become a more unified field with a central focus (chapter two), that grading, testing and assessing student writing are separate acts incorrectly lumped together and that makes us miss the importance of assessment for the teaching of writing (chapter three), that all assessment practice contains theoretical implications (chapter four), that responding to student writing should focus more on the way we read student work and write back to them (chapter five), that assessment has been developed as a technology and can benefit greatly from being revised as research (chapter six), and that writing assessment can never be understood outside of its practical applications (chapter seven) are less a re-imagining than they are a way of seeing something old and familiar as something new and novel. It is in this spirit that I came to call this volume *(Re)Articulating Writing Assessment for Teaching and Learning.* I do think that the individual chapters I mention above and about which I will elaborate more fully can add up to a new understanding of writing assessment. My purpose in writing this volume was to look at the various ways in which assessment is currently constructed and to articulate a new identity for writing assessment scholars and scholarship.

(RE) ARTICULATION

Before I outline the basic tenets that guide this volume, its scope, what the reader can expect throughout and how the various chapters work toward its overall purpose, it is important to talk about what I mean by (re)articulating writing assessment and even what I mean by the term "assessment"—what it is I hope to explain about assessment's connection to teaching and learning, why in some ways I think we need to reframe assessment for its pedagogical value, and why I think writing assessment has never been fully connected to teaching. I chose "articulation" as the *what* I wanted to do for assessment in this volume because it describes a kind of attention assessment needs but has never received. We need to talk about assessment in new ways, to recognize how ubiquitous it is within the process of reading and writing. Since we are constantly making judgments about the texts we read, we need to see how our judgments about texts get articulated into specific assessments or evaluations (terms I use interchangeably throughout the volume) and how these articulations affect students and the learning environment. My use of "(re)" illustrates that assessment has been articulated already, and that part of my work is to articulate it in new ways. It is not entirely clear to me that assessment has ever been articulated in ways advocated here—ways that support rather than detract from the teaching and learning of writing. I use the parentheses around "(re)" to indicate this ambiguity.

As is already clear in my discussion of articulation, assessment can be used to mean many things. I wish I had some definitive idea of how we could define assessment. Of course, we could point to some limited notion of the word as being involved with evaluating the performance or value of a particular event, object, or idea. This limited definition, though, it seems to me, misses the larger impact of our judgments and would not necessarily be focused within the context of school, or more specifically, the teaching of writing. It is one thing for me to read a piece of writing and say whether or not I like it. It's another thing for me to make that statement in the classroom or on a student's paper. I would contend that the type of classroom, subject, level of instruction, and other contextual factors would further define what impact my statement of value would have on an individual or others interested in that individual. The role I have or my identity in each of these situations also influences how someone might take or respond to my judgment. I remember my daughter being in third or fourth grade and having me help her with a paper she was writing. It took a little effort for me to actually convince her that she could improve her writing by having someone respond to it and then rewriting. She received an A+ on that particular paper and for awhile would exclaim to everyone how she was going to let me read her writing and revise accordingly (my word not hers) because I had helped her get so high a grade. Although she knew what I did for a living, it really carried no weight with her. It was only after she had actually profited from my judgment and advice that she would actually seek it, something I might add that she no longer does. My role as her father did not automatically identify me as an expert to her. On the other hand, as an instructor in a writing classroom, I am often aware of the great impact my judgment about writing could have on a particular student or the entire class. I also understand that the attention students accord my judgments is not unrelated to my role as the grade-giver in the class.

The idea that we as teachers may often not wish to state a specific judgment leads me to consider that an assessment in the formal sense may be more than just a specific judgment, but rather an articulation of that judgment. The form and the context of the articulation gives us some other ways to think and talk about a new understanding for assessment. Certainly, a statement I might make in class about something I value in writing or in a specific text could impact my students thinking or cause them to take up a specific action. For example, Warren Combs and William L. Smith (1980) found that although students in a course that emphasized sentence combining would write sentences with a greater number of T-units, students without sentence combining instruction would produce similar sentences by just being told that the teacher/examiner liked longer sentences. In other words, our statements as teachers in the context of a class can have a great deal of power or influence over students. Grades are probably the best example of this. Giving students an A or even a

B, even when we suggest revision, probably doesn't encourage them to revise, because the grade itself carries more weight as an evaluation than what we can say about revision. While grades are but one kind of evaluation we can give students, they tend to carry more weight than other assessment articulations because they are more formal and codified. Grades are part of a larger system of values that have been used to identify or label people. In education, grades are a totalizing evaluative mechanism. It is common for people to sum up their experiences as students by saying, "I was an A or C student." In recent years, it has become common to see bumper stickers that proclaim "My son or daughter is an A student at [blank] School," as if this says something inherently good about that child or his or her parents.

It's important to note that while we may give a grade for many different reasons, what ends up getting articulated becomes a part of that larger system of values that has weight and influence far beyond the evaluative judgment we have initially made. Moves, then, to articulate our value judgments about student work in different ways illustrate the separation that exists between the judgment(s) we make and the statement(s) we can make about those judgments. These principles also apply to tests about writing that function outside the classroom. In fact, we might argue that assessment outside the classroom is even more formal and more codified than that within the classroom. For example, in placement testing we actually decide for a student where she will be placed for the next fifteen weeks or, perhaps even more importantly, where she will begin her college or university level writing instruction. Other writing assessments have similar power and can allow or prevent students from entering certain programs or receiving a certain credential. While we can base our judgments of student writing upon many different features, we can also articulate those judgments in different ways, and both the judgments and their articulation can have profound effects upon students and their ability to succeed. Furthermore, the articulation of judgment can easily be codified and assigned cultural value. I am reminded of the story one of my students told me about his two daughters. In the state of Kentucky, students submit writing portfolios as part of a state assessment program. The portfolios are assigned one of four scale points, but instead of using numbers, the scale is divided into Distinguished, Proficient, Apprentice, and Novice. During an argument the two children were having, one of them replied, "What do you know, you're only a novice."

If assessment consists of the judgments we make about student writing ability, the form these judgments can take, and the context within which these judgments are made, then a new articulation for assessment requires that we attend to both the way we make the judgments and the form of our statement(s) about them. Important to this understanding is a consciousness about the level of formality different articulations can take and what influence they can have. In defining assessment as both judgment and the articulation of that judgment, I am specifically interested in neutralizing assessment's more negative influences and accentuating its more positive effects for teaching and learning. Just as Samuel Messick's (1989b) theory of validity includes building a rationale for assessing in the first place, I think we need to examine why we might want to communicate a specific judgment to students or others about a student's writing—what possible educational value would such an articulation serve for this particular student at this pedagogical moment?

Actually, my intention to (re)articulate writing assessment as a positive, important aspect of designing, administrating and theorizing writing instruction has its roots in early conceptions of assessment as progressive social action. The idea of assessment as social action is not new. Since its inception in ancient China, assessment was supposed to disrupt existing social order and class systems (Hanson 1993). However, as we all know, assessment has rarely delivered on this promise. Instead, assessment has been used as an interested social mechanism for reinscribing current power relations and class systems.

This overall negative impression of assessment is exacerbated in composition, since one of the driving impulses in the formulation of composition as an area of study in the 1970s was against current-traditional rhetorical practices that emphasized correctness and the assessment methods to enforce it. One of the responses from the composition community to the negative effects of assessment has been to avoid assessment altogether. One of the results of composition's avoidance of assessment issues has been that major procedures for assessment like holistic scoring were developed by testing companies based upon theoretical and epistemological positions that do not reflect current knowledge of literacy and its teaching. If we can influence and change the agenda for social action in tests and testing, we can change writing assessment. Constructing an agenda for writing assessment as social action means connecting assessment to teaching, something people like Edward White (1994) and Richard Lloyd-Jones (1977), among others, have been advocating for nearly three decades. Instead of envisioning assessment as a way to enforce certain culturally positioned standards and refuse entrance to certain people and groups of people, we need to use our assessments to aid the learning environment for both teachers and students.

Because assessment is the site where we marshal evidence about what we will value globally as a society and more locally as teachers, researchers and administrators, we can, by changing assessment, change what we will ultimately value. It is no secret that most standardized tests as well as local judgments about academic achievement or aptitude are biased. Women and minorities, for example, score lower on certain tests, even though there may no real reason to question their ability and achievement. We can label such tests biased, and some tests do issue point values in calculating the disadvantage a certain person may have on a particular test. We can even adjust our judgment based upon this form of social action because, like affirmative action, the assumption is that scoring poorly on a certain test doesn't mean a person doesn't deserve a particular opportunity. On the other hand, this kind of affirmative or social action implies deficit. Since affirmative action is increasingly under fire, it is time we visited fully the impact of assessments upon minorities, so that instead of adjusting test results, we could use tests that are fair to all. What if the tests themselves were changed, so that students of higher income-level parents, for example, wouldn't receive a disproportionate number of the higher scores? This not only eliminates the bias in the current assessment, but it also changes the public evidence about what is valuable—ultimately influencing not only our perception of merit but also our perception of who the bright and capable people are in this country. An agenda for assessment that recognizes it as an important element for social action allows us the ability to guard against over-privileging the values, gestures and customs of certain groups and provides assessment with the potential to become an agent for progressive social change that includes and highlights the improvement of educational environments and opportunities for all students.

Although the potential for assessment is large, its overall track record is dismal. Students and teachers have seldom recognized or been able to harness its potential to improve teaching and learning. In fact, assessment has often been seen as a negative, disruptive feature for the teaching of writing. The quote below from an issue of *English Journal* is typical of this attitude:

> This is not a topic the present editors would have chosen to focus on in their last issue of *English Journal*. Nor is its placement immediately after a section on romanticism particularly appropriate. Assessment is not our favorite subject. (*English Journal* 1994, 37)

This stance toward assessment, of course, is understandable given the lack of input from teachers in outside assessment and the punitive and pervasive nature of assessment in current traditional writing classrooms, a point I explore in chapter three where I argue for the use of assessment as a viable classroom strategy for the teaching of writing. One of the overall goals of this book is to create new attitudes toward assessment that can help harness its power for teaching and learning. Much of what is wrong with assessment, both in the way it is conceived within the teaching of writing and in the practices of assessment outside the classroom for programmatic, institutional, or political purposes, can be traced back to the lack of attention to assessment as a viable and legitimate part of the teaching of writing. As I argue in chapter three, people who write well have the ability to assess their own writing, and if we are to teach students to write successfully, then we have to teach them to assess their own writing.

It may very well be that much of the tumult surrounding the teaching of writing during the twentieth century, and in particular the recent backlash against certain theories and methods, might be related to the neglected status of theory and practice in writing assessment. Foucault (1977) and scholars in composition (Fitzgerald 1996; O'Neill 1998; Traschel 1992) argue that assessment is an essential factor in disciplinary formation. In fact, the argument could be made that composition as a discipline owes its initiation to the written examinations established by postsecondary institutions in the late nineteenth century. The shaping influence of assessment on composition cannot be underestimated. Both Peggy O'Neill (1998) and Mary Traschel (1992) make strong arguments concerning its central role. Our failure to pay enough attention to the role of evaluation has had far ranging implications beyond the development of adequate practices for writing assessment. We have failed not only to address the role of writing assessment in the ways we teach and write, but we have subsequently failed to theorize this influence at all. In a recent discussion of Stephen North's *The Making of Knowledge in Composition,* James Zebroski (1998) notes that North's inquiry into the way knowledge is made starts with the results of a doctoral examination. While Zebroski questions the origins of such an inquiry, it makes perfect sense to begin to look at how and where knowledge gets made based upon a moment of examination in which the values of individuals and the institutions they represent are most visible. Zebroski's problem with North's beginning is but one more example of the way assessment is undervalued. Foucault (1977) asserts that the examination is imbricated in disciplinary formation and identity. This relationship between assessment and identity and value in education is well articulated in Lauren Resnick and David Resnick's (1992) contention that if we don't test for something it will disappear from the curriculum. We need to articulate a much more conscious, theoretical and practical link between the way we think about assessment and the way we think about the teaching, research and theorizing of writing, recognizing that assessment is a vital component in the act of writing, in the teaching of writing, and in the ways we define our students, courses and programs. Because assessment is a direct representation of what we value and how we assign that value, it says much about our identities as teachers, researchers and theorists. This recognition of the importance and centrality of assessment will require a major rethinking of the role and importance of assessment in our theories, teaching, and research.

Assessment can and should be not only an important component of a healthy research and administrative agenda but also an integral, important and vital part of the effective teaching of writing. One of the main goals of this book is to establish the importance of assessment to the teaching of writing and to connect the teaching of writing to what we now call writing assessment. A common assumption about the teaching of writing and its assessment is that there is a lack of fit between the way we assess and the way we teach. A basic tenet of this volume is that similar assumptions and beliefs about assigning value to student writing permeate both our classroom and programmatic ideas about and procedures for assessing student writing. For this reason, I address assessment in this volume both in and outside the classroom. And, perhaps even more importantly, these beliefs and assumptions remain largely uncritical and unexamined. The act of articulating the many ways assessment permeates practices in and outside the classroom can help make our assumptions more visible, enabling us to revise assessment in the service of teaching and learning.

The relationship of assessing and teaching writing is at once complex and conflicted. While the gaps between theory and practice are a fact of life in most, if not all, applied disciplines like composition, the split between the two seems especially prominent in writing assessment. For example, at the 1999 Conference on College Composition and Communication (CCCC), there were few sessions devoted to writing assessment and even fewer devoted to assessing writing outside of the classroom. However, there were over 150 people who attended a Thursday morning session on assessment as social action and again that many people were present at the last session of the conference, also on assessment—more people, I am told, than attended a featured session that morning with a prominent scholar. It appears that while this historical moment finds few scholars interested in assessment, more and more of us are pressed to find out all we can on short notice to answer a mandate for assessment at our home institutions. At any rate, the need, if not the interest, for (re)articulating assessment is readily apparent. I explore some of the assumptions behind common scenarios for assessment in chapter seven, as I examine what I think is some confusion about exactly what constitutes assessment practice and theory. I contend that critical-reflective examinations and the consciousness they promote can only blur theory-practice boundaries. At a workshop I conducted a year or so ago, a participant who had already begun an assessment project remarked that most literature on writing assessment was theoretical. I responded that I thought the opposite was true, something the literature supports, since it has been common to assume that we have been too busy answering practical concerns to construct a theoretical basis for writing assessment (Cherry and Witte 1998; Faigley, Cherry, Jolliffe and Skinner 1985; Gere 1980). I also remember that this participant resisted any advice I could offer about conceptualizing or theorizing her efforts. She had already begun to collect data about teacher perceptions of student writing and wanted to know what to do with this information—a question that probably should have been worked out conceptually and theoretically in the planning stages. It is often difficult to interest those in throes of assessment with any theoretical considerations, though it is only by emphasizing the link between theory and practice, and the reflective, critical conscious it engenders, that any substantive change in writing assessment practice can be accomplished.

In giving workshops, attending sessions at CCCCs and other conferences, and talking with those in attendance, I am struck by the pressure that many in our profession are feeling to implement assessment procedures for a variety of reasons. As Kathleen Yancey (1999) points out in her history of writing assessment and CCCC, program assessment may be the new wave in writing assessment. If, as Yancey (1999) contends, "historicizing" writing assessment is important in helping us avoid the mistakes of the past, then it is imperative that we not only become involved in designing and developing assessment procedures, but that we take the lead in integrating assessment into our profession and our lives as writing teachers and program administrators. Our profession's abandonment of assessment as a positive practice and its adaptation of negative conceptions of assessment as punitive and counterproductive to fostering literate behavior in our students cannot but continue to put us in a position of powerlessness, while at the same time putting our students and programs in peril. To come to a new understanding of assessment is to not only become conscious of its importance, power, and necessity for literacy and its teaching, but also to understand assessment as one of our ethical and professional responsibilities (Beason 2000).

The scope of this book then, is purposefully ambitious—one of its basic goals is to change the way assessment is thought of by the people who teach writing, administer writing programs, and work in educational measurement. Any complete transformation of writing assessment identity is obviously beyond the scope of an individual volume. However, this book attempts to begin such a transformation and is, therefore, fundamentally different from most recent work devoted to writing assessment. For example, a recent volume in writing assessment (White, Lutz, and Kamuskiri 1996) includes contributors from composition and the measurement community and enters new territory in addressing the political aspects of writing assessment. However, the overall message of this recent volume is not new. There is a continuing faith in the technology of testing: "The technical apparatus of assessment is important; its quality determines whether the information it yields can be trusted" (Camp 1996, 99). While there is some truth in this statement, I believe it is time to move beyond this complete and largely unwarranted faith in the technology of testing to create site-based and locally controlled assessments of writing, as I explore in chapter four. Only by focusing on the local decision-making process can we heed the call from validity theorists to validate each use of a test (Cronbach 1988; Messick 1989a; 1989b; Moss 1992; Shepard 1993). This volume heeds the call of White, Lutz, and Kamuskiri: "The future of writing assessment requires that we articulate a theoretical basis for our assessment practices" (1996, 105). In chapter four, I begin by articulating the beliefs and assumptions inherent in traditional writing assessment and contrast it with work done at a few schools in which assessment programs have been designed outside the theoretical umbrella normally associated with assessment. The attention to portfolios and the many volumes to come out of this attention (Belanoff and Dickson 1991; Black, Daiker, Sommers, and Stygall 1994; Murphy and Underwood, 2000; Sunstein and Lovell, 2000; Yancey 1992; and others) have all called for looking at assessment in new ways, ways shaped and defined by the portfolio. The portfolio movement remains one of the most important catalysts for real change and growth in writing assessment. However, most attempts to use portfolios outside the classroom have involved their standardization along with other technologies of testing important to a positivist, traditional approach to assessment that consolidates power and control with a central authority and away from teachers and their immediate supervisors (Berlak 1992; Broad 2000; Callahan 1997a; 1997b; 1999; Huot and Williamson 1997; Murphy 1994; 1997). Unless we look beyond specific practices to the theories and histories that drive all assessment practices, we will fail to reap the potential of portfolios, or any other measures, to substantively change the way writing is assessed.

In chapter two, I attempt to look at the possibility of seeing writing assessment as a unified field. As I outline the ways in which writing assessment has been constructed by various scholars, it becomes apparent that, for the most part, work in writing assessment gets done by college-level writing scholars with connections to the field of composition or by scholars connected to educational measurement who work on issues germane to K–12. I argue that both groups of scholars have much to gain by connecting their work into a more coherent field of study and in using more current conceptions of validity to hold this joint venture together. This chapter begins in earnest an attempt to (re)articulate a field of writing assessment in which those working in isolation can connect with each other and create not only a new, unified field but the possibilities for increased attention to writing assessment and its ability to enhance teaching and learning.

In chapter three, I focus on assessment that occurs within a writing classroom. My main point is that although grading, testing, and assessing writing are quite distinct from one another and have quite different implications, we have often lumped them together. I argue that teaching students how to assess their own writing (as distinct from assessing their progress as students) is an important facet in teaching students how to write. This chapter emphasizes the importance of understanding the different ways we can assess our students and the importance of the implications for each kind of assessment. Distinguishing between the ways we can articulate our judgments about writing, on the one hand, and the impact these articulations can have on students and the writing classroom, on the other, illustrates the important role assessment can have for students learning to write as they struggle to understand the power and potential of their own abilities to articulate judgment about writing.

In chapter four, I explore the beliefs and assumptions behind the practices of writing assessment. I do this historically, looking back at the ways writing assessment practices have been developed through the years, acknowledging the philosophical and epistemological debts of these practices. This is a longer, revised version of an essay that appeared in the December, 1996 issue of *College Composition and Communication (CCC)*. Joseph Harris, then editor of *CCC*, and at least one of the reviewers wanted a tighter focus in the original essay that looked only at college-level issues and did not focus so much on the history of the practices. I contended then, and I contend now, that we cannot talk about the theoretical implications of writing assessment without a larger focus. I argue in chapter four that it is impossible to effect any substantive changes in writing assessment unless we address underlying theoretical and epistemological issues as well.

In chapter five, I write about the act of responding to student writing. In reviewing most of the literature on response, I come to the conclusion that we have focused, for the most part, on developing different ways to respond to student writing and on detailing advice for teachers to respond better to their students. While these are certainly important and laudatory aims, the response literature seems stunted, since it has neglected to look at the obvious fact that to respond to student writing we must first read it. I argue that the act of reading itself is an important constraint on the kinds of meaning we can make of student texts and the responses we can construct based on our reading. I conclude the chapter by noting that just as our response is affected by our reading, so too it depends upon our ability to craft a rhetorically reasonable and coherent message to our students. As Richard Miller (1994) and Louise Phelps (2000) have both noted, response to student writing is a crucial and neglected topic in composition scholarship. I hope this chapter can encourage an increased attention to response and its importance for the teaching of writing.

Chapter six focuses on the ways in which writing assessment has been developed and constructed as a technology. Drawing upon the work of George Madhaus (1993), who builds a compelling argument for educational assessment as a technological apparatus, I articulate how writing assessment is a technology and how this technology creates the problems inherent in a technological focus for writing assessment. Contrasting this technological focus, I propose that we come to understand writing assessment as research. Building upon an understanding of writing assessment as research, I argue that there are many benefits in constructing writing assessment in this new way. Seeing assessment as research can create new roles for those of us who work in writing assessment while at the same time creating a new vision for assessment that is focused on answering important questions asked by specific communities of teachers, students and scholars.

Chapter seven focuses on writing assessment practice. I begin with the apparent contradiction of having been distinguished as a theorist on one hand but having my theoretical work labeled as practical. This chapter is a fitting close for the volume in which I explore just how practical, self-conscious, and reflective all writing assessment work should and can be. We must become aware of our beliefs and assumptions while at the same time we attend to the practical pressure of assessment. I argue that all of us who teach writing and administer writing assessment programs need to practice assessment on a conscious, theoretical, and reflective level. Only with a tangible commitment to assessment and a conscious awareness of the beliefs and assumptions inherent in these practices can we avoid theory/practice splits and learn to harness the power of theoretically grounded assessment practices.

Throughout this volume, I hope to build upon emergent and alternative research, theory, and practice to create a methodology for writing teachers, writing program administrators, and assessment professionals to establish practices that recognize and support the importance of contextual, institutional, and local standards. Considering the pressures that writing teachers and writing program administrators face in developing and implementing writing assessment at their respective institutions along with the neglected status of writing assessment both as a theoretical and practical enterprise, it is crucial that we begin the development of a new methodology. It must be a methodology with which those who teach writing and administer writing programs can learn to appreciate the importance of assessment and to translate their concerns for their students and programs into solid knowledge-producing assessments that meet the needs of outside pressures and enrich teaching and programs from within as well.

The purpose of this book, then, is to change the way writing teachers, writing program administrators, and writing assessment professionals think about teaching and assessing student writing. In the assessment community, it is common to distinguish between summative assessment, which is final and at the end of a project or performance, and formative assessment, which is made while a project or performance is still in progress. The distinction assumes that formative types of assessment are less rigid and punitive and allow for adjustments and improvement based upon the assessment. In writing assessment, it might be wise to include *instructive assessment* (a term I explore more fully in chapter three) because the assessment of student progress is a constant part of the composing process in which writers return to their writing as they attempt to compose new pieces of text, pushing forward while they revise and move ahead. This connection between assessment and instruction as exemplified in the notion of instructive assessment is part of a larger movement in educational assessment that recognizes the importance of holding all educational practices, including assessment, to rigorous standards that include the enhancement of teaching and learning. Validity theorists like Lee Cronbach (1989) and Samuel Messick (1989a; 1989b) stipulated over several decades that in order for a measurement to have some degree of validity, decisions made on its behalf must have a positive effect on the educational environment. For writing assessment, this would mean that all procedures used to assess writing would also contain properties that work toward the improvement of the teaching and learning of writing.

In addition to its ambitious scope, this volume also attempts to reach a far-ranging audience because, while the book works to create the type of theory necessary for transforming writing assessment practice, the message of such a text is that writing assessment must be site-based and locally controlled, and that writing teachers and program administrators must begin to see writing assessment as part of their jobs, a point I make throughout this introduction and the entire volume. Reaching writing program administrators (WPAs) is a vital concern for this book, because in order for assessment to truly change, we must involve those who regularly oversee the day-to-day operations for writing centers; composition, technical, and professional communication programs; and writing across the curriculum programs. This book hopes to help WPAs as a network of writing assessment professionals to see assessment and administration as mutually inclusive and important to the design and maintenance of programs that effectively teach students to write for a wide range of audiences and purposes. Writing teachers and WPAs are often responsible for such common writing assessment practices as first-year college placement, exit or proficiency exams at the first- or third-year level, as well as program assessment for composition and/or writing across the curriculum programs. These practitioners often lack even the most rudimentary preparation. A survey of first-year college placement shows that a large majority of people in charge of such programs have no previous experience or training in writing assessment or composition (Huot 1994a).

While this book should be accessible to practitioners who are interested in writing assessment, especially WPAs, it is also directed at writing assessment researchers and theorists who are interested in pushing the theoretical and practical envelope about writing assessment. The small handful of schools who have experimented with assessment practices have been watched by the rest of the assessing and teaching writing communities. These experimental procedures along with innovations like using portfolios for placement or exemption are important to this volume and create an extended audience of assessment researchers who read and write for each other.

Lastly, I want to reemphasize the importance of writing teachers and those who educate them as a potential audience for this book. My message to teachers is that the proper and intelligent use of assessment can provide them with an opportunity to learn rich, useful information about their students, pedagogy, and programs. I address such a wide range not just to encourage potential readers but to emphasize that one of the purposes of this volume is to create an interest in and an audience for assessment that has yet to exist. This book attempts to build a *new assessment*, demystifying traditional notions of assessment as a privatized technical apparatus and focusing on the role of writing teachers and administrators and their expertise. This new assessment not only links pedagogy with evaluation practices, it makes the ability to assess one's own writing a primary goal of the teaching and learning of writing. Understanding the power of well-designed, site-based and locally controlled writing assessment procedures guards against the use of any unnecessary, standardized or large-scale current traditional assessments. Ultimately, this volume is about understanding the power of assessment for classroom and programmatic purposes, for harnessing that power to the beliefs and assumptions that drive our pedagogies, and for controlling that power in a productive fashion for the teaching and learning of writing.

2
WRITING ASSESSMENT AS A FIELD OF STUDY

It is becoming more and more clear to me that the work that I and others do in writing assessment, like work in other fields, is constrained, shaped and promoted by the overall shape of the field itself, yet writing assessment—as a field—has not been the object of inquiry for very much scholarship. There are several reasons for this, of course. Writing assessment researchers have been busy doing other things, mainly trying to establish procedures that could measure student ability in writing. Although research into the assessment of writing goes back to the early part of this century (Starch and Eliott 1912), there really hasn't been much of a sense that writing assessment was, indeed, a field of study. Most work in assessment before the 1970s was carried out within the field of educational measurement, which still considers writing as just one more area of research within its vast domain of all educational testing. Interest and activity in writing assessment, however, has changed radically since the 1970s. In the last three decades, there has been much research and inquiry into writing assessment issues, enough by the early 1990s to support the establishment of a journal, *Assessing Writing*, devoted entirely to the assessment of student writing, and more recently a second periodical, *The Journal of Writing Assessment*.

Writing assessment has evolved into an intellectual and public site in which scholarship is conceived and implemented by people from various disciplines and subdisciplines. In a 1990 review,

I was able to identify three main foci for the existent literature in writing assessment: topic development and task selection, text and writing quality, and influences of rater judgment on writing quality (Huot 1990). I had attempted to let the issues covered in the literature itself focus the review and discussion, being very careful in choosing the three areas around which most scholarship in writing assessment clustered. Just four years later, in introducing the new journal *Assessing Writing* (Huot 1994c), I noted that none of the articles in our first issue dealt with the three major themes evident in the literature review four years earlier. The fact that areas of interest change in a given field of study is not by itself a significant point. However, what I noted then and bears repeating now is that scholarship in writing assessment up until the 1990s was mostly concerned with establishing the procedures themselves. While the landmark study conducted by Godshalk, Swineford and Coffman and published in 1966 outlined the procedures necessary to produce agreement among independent raters, the scholarship for the next twenty-five years or so focused on how to maintain the efficacy of these procedures (White 1994), as well as how to solve technical problems like the creation of similar topics for tests that attempted to compare scores from one year to another (Hoetker 1982), or how to train raters to agree and then statistically compute this agreement (Myers 1980). What's important to highlight in a chapter on writing assessment as an area of study is that while the literature up until the early 1990s focused on establishing and maintaining writing assessment procedures, more recent work has begun to critique current traditional writing assessment practices.

In her recent history of writing assessment, Kathleen Yancey (1999) notes that much writing assessment in the 1950s and 1960s was conducted through the use of multiple choice tests of grammar, usage and mechanics. Although essays had been used since the nineteenth century to test writing ability (Connors 1986; Traschel 1992), they had always been held suspect by the educational measurement community because of the low consistency of agreement between independent raters—what is termed *interrater reliability*. As early as 1912, essay testing was proclaimed problematic because it was unreliable (Starch and Elliott 1912). It was not until 1941, however, under the pressure to test and matriculate students for World War II, that the College Board actually did away with essay testing (Fuess 1967). The establishment of the reliable procedures of holistic, primary trait, and analytic scoring for writing assessment in the 1960s and early 1970s was no small feat, and the attendant optimism it generated is understandable (Cooper 1977; White 1994). This optimism continued up into the 1990s, as most of the literature on writing assessment attempted to establish and maintain its legitimacy as a valid and reliable form of direct writing assessment. This reckoning of how the study of writing assessment is constituted is especially important for an area like writing assessment, since it is a subject that draws interest from a diverse group of people, from classroom instructors to writing program administrators, to school and universities officials, to state and federal legislators, to testing companies and assessment scholars, not to mention students and parents. Add to the conflicting interests of these groups the fact that work in writing assessment can come from different fields and various subfields with different and conflicting theoretical and epistemological orientations, and we get a picture of writing assessment as a field pulled in many directions by competing interests, methods and orientations.

TWO DIFFERENT DISCIPLINES

In understanding writing assessment as a field of study, perhaps the most significant issue is that many of the scholars involved represent different disciplines that hold differing and often conflicting epistemological and theoretical positions. Composition, of course, is a field that welcomes and uses knowledge from various fields and disciplines. However, in writing assessment, we not only borrow and use knowledge, but scholars from education and the measurement community consider writing assessment as their area of study as well. In fact, we are all in debt to the measurement community for the most commonly used forms of writing assessment. Although Edward White (1993) and Kathleen Yancey (1999) write about developing or importing procedures from ETS, holistic scoring is essentially the same procedure *developed by* CEEB and ETS. It's important to note that while the reintroduction of essay scoring in the early 1970s was seen as a real breakthrough for composition and English teachers (White 1994, 1993; Yancey 1999), in reality it was the culmination of decades worth of research by the educational measurement community who had been grappling with the problem of reliability since the early part of the century. While I applaud the work that produced holistic and analytic scoring and the movement to use student writing in assessing student writing ability, it's important to see holistic scoring in two ways. The English teaching profession vociferously protested English and writing tests that contained no writing (Fuess, 1967; Palmer, 1960) and promoted continued research into essay scoring that culminated in the research (Godshalk, Swineford and Coffman, 1966) that produced acceptable rates of interrater reliability. However, no English or composition scholars played a major role in the development of holistic scoring. It was a procedure devised to ensure reliable scoring among independent readers, since reliability as a "necessary but insufficient condition for validity" (Cherry and Meyer 1993, 110) is a cornerstone of traditional measurement that spawned multiple choice tests and the entire testing culture and mentality that has become such an important part of current ideas about education. Although the advent of holistic scoring permitted student writing to once again be part of the tests in English and writing, we must not lose sight of the fact that holistic scoring is a product of the same thinking that produced the indirect tests of grammar, usage and mechanics. That is, like multiple choice tests, holistic scoring was developed to produce reliable scores.

Perhaps it's best to understand writing assessment as an area of study that is, at least in the ideal, interdisciplinary. I say ideal because interdisciplinarity involves an integration and dialectic that has not been present in writing assessment study, though the type of borrowing across disciplines that sometimes occurs in writing assessment scholarship has at times been labeled inter-disciplinary (Klein 1990). It might be best to call the scholarship in writing assessment *multi*disciplinary, since it has taken place within various disciplines. The idea of writing assessment exist-ing across disciplinary boundaries is probably not new, though there is little crossover of scholars and work. For example, in 1990 I published two essays on writing assessment, one in *College Composition and Communication*, the flagship journal for composi-tion, and the other in *Review of Educational Research*, a journal published by the American Educational Research Association, the major organization for educational researchers. Invariably, I have found that within a specific article either one or the other piece would be cited. Very few people ever referred to both, and of course it was easy once I saw which piece was cited to know what field of study the writer(s) represented. This example illus-trates the lack of integration of scholarship within writing assess-ment. Writing assessment scholarship occurs in two academic forums, and the lack of connection between the two is a notion that we have yet to address in writing assessment literature because this literature has been written and read by those within a specific field who have little or no knowledge or interest in the other approach.

Edward White's essay, "Issues and Problems in Writing Assessment" (1994b) notes that people who work in writing assess-ment often have very different orientations toward testing and education. White's list of those with an interest in writing assess-ment: "writing teachers, researchers and theorists, testing firms and governmental bodies, students, minorities and other margin-alized groups" underscores his point that the interests and approaches of the various factions in writing assessment put cer-tain claims on what kind of assessments we should design and how these assessments should be used. This version of the field seems to be in line with the notion of the "stakeholder," assessment talk for all of those who have a claim on a specific assessment. In

White's view, each group competes with other groups for preeminence. While he gives some sense of the various tensions writing assessment needs to address, his categories dwell on the individual roles people play within the area of writing assessment and the needs and claims these roles suggest, without taking into account the larger social, disciplinary and historical factors that help to create the tensions he discusses, which in turn make writing assessment the field it is. It is fair to note that White's purposes in outlining the various people who may work in writing assessment and the various concerns that these people bring with them are different from my purposes here, since I'm interested in the makeup of the field itself. However, White's approach does have implications for the ways we think of the field. If writing assessment, as White suggests, is a field made up of various individuals who have differing and conflicting interests, then one implication is that we need to create a venue or forum that allows all of these concerns to be heard and addressed—which is exactly what White suggests at the conclusion of his article. This picture of the field and its suggestion for the future is not unlike the one depicted by Yancey's (1999) recent history in which she urges the balancing of reliability and validity as a way to reconcile disparate forces in writing assessment.

To understand the forces that both Yancey and White identify in their own ways, we need to look at the larger social, historical and disciplinary factors that comprise the field of writing assessment. Educational measurement is an area of study that can trace its roots back to the early decades of the twentieth century when researchers struggled not only to design and administer the first educational tests but also to establish the viability of the idea that there were, indeed, educational achievements and aptitudes that could actually be measured. This movement in educational measurement and its scholarship was closely allied to work in psychology which was also trying to establish the viability of certain human psychological traits that could also be defined and tested. The need to establish the viability and legitimacy of these enterprises and the fields themselves drove both educational and psychological measurement scholars to consider emerging statistical procedures from the physical sciences. It's important to recall the intellectual climate of the early twentieth century and its focus on empirical, measurable, physical, human phenomena. Hence, the use of numerical explanations developed into the attendant field of psychometrics that attempts to understand human phenomena statistically. The connection between educational and psychological measurement can still be seen in the American Psychological Association (APA) *Standards for Testing*, which is published periodically and serves as a handbook for both educational and psychological testing and testers. It should be pointed out that although these standards are published by APA, the teams of scholars who write the standards come from both the educational and psychological testing communities. The field of educational psychology is an example of the interdisciplinary connections between these two fields. It should also be noted that scholars trained in educational psychology often work on questions regarding students literate practices and publish in journals devoted to English language education (Hilgers 1984, 1986; Shumacher and Nash, 1991), connecting educational psychology with the work done by education and composition scholars.

To understand the connection of writing assessment to the field of educational measurement, we probably should also understand its connection to the field of psychology. Recognizing these connections is crucial if we are to understand the theories behind current traditional writing assessment procedures like holistic, analytic, and primary trait scoring. Although I explore the nature of these theories more fully in chapter four as they relate to specific assessment practices, it's important to note that when Pamela Moss (1998) and others from educational measurement (Breland 1996) criticize college writing assessment, they are doing it from a theoretical perspective at odds with those I who work in composition. For if the educational measurement community is closely allied with the field of psychology, those who approach writing assessment from composition are allied with scholars in literary theory (Bakhtin 1981) critical theory

(Foucault 1977) and composition (Berlin 1988; Bizzell 1992; Faigley 1992). Just as important as the nature of these theories is the object of inquiry. For as educational measurement and psychology focus on sampling techniques, statistical trends and concepts like reliability and validity, composition looks at the importance of context and the processes of reading and writing and their teaching. It's safe to say, then, that White's categories of those who work in writing assessment contain individuals whose interests are shaped by certain theoretical and epistemological orientations and whose methods and approaches are determined by specific disciplinary allegiances. For example, when Yancey urges the balancing of reliability and validity, what she is really advocating is that those with different concerns for writing assessment, like English teachers and assessment specialists, work in harmony with each other. There is of course a certain logical, not to mention political, appeal to what White and Yancey see as the field of writing assessment and the collaboration they advocate. After all, if we are all stakeholders in writing assessment with our own competing claims, it is only by working together that we can honor these disparate claims.

The approaches to writing assessment advocated by educational measurement and college composition scholars are not only based upon different theories and epistemologies, but these approaches also value different aspects of an assessment. These different foci are recognized by large and reputable testing companies like the Educational Testing Service (ETS) and American College Testing (ACT) who regularly hire "content" staff who, for the purposes of writing assessment, have training and experience in literature, creative writing and/or the teaching of writing and language education. For the most part, content staffers in educational testing companies earn less than those trained in educational measurement, while those with backgrounds in educational or psychological measurement occupy supervisory and policy-making positions. In the world of professional writing assessment, then, there is some recognition of the need for information and expertise about the teaching of writing, but that information is secondary to information about technical and statistical properties of developing, administering and interpreting writing assessments. This emphasis on the technical aspects of writing assessment visible in the structure of testing companies is also part of the literature on writing assessment (Breland 1996; Camp 1996; Scharton 1996) in which the technical aspects of writing assessment are emphasized, and English teachers' opinions about and efforts with writing assessment are criticized (Breland 1996; Scharton 1996). This criticism of college writing assessment by those with an interest and background in educational assessment signals that the work in college writing assessment by those with backgrounds in English and composition is at least starting to attract some attention by the educational measurement community, even if it is critical.

ISOLATION

Writing assessment has over the last three decades become a field in which scholarship takes place in different disciplines, and these two disciplines, college English and educational measurement, have different orientations, produce different kinds of assessments and are often in conflict about what constitutes appropriate writing assessment. The work of Pamela Moss, who is situated in educational measurement, has been used recently by people working in college writing assessment primarily because she has begun to challenge the status quo about reliability in her article "Can There be Validity Without Reliability" (1994a). More recently, in responding to Richard Haswell's scheme for validating program assessment, she notes that "Professor Haswell paints a picture of the field of college writing assessment that appears seriously isolated from the larger educational assessment community" (1998, 113). Like White, Moss sees writing assessment as an area of study in which different people pursue their own agenda, asking different questions and using different methods. Unlike White, however, Moss's notion of writing assessment is set in terms of disciplinary connections. Instead of pointing out various individuals who work

in assessment, her point about Haswell and others who work in
college writing assessment is based upon their connections to a
specific discipline. Haswell's work, Moss contends, could be
made stronger were he to use approaches, principles and concepts from educational measurement. Moss's statement con-
firms the division in writing assessment between educational
measurement and the college assessment communities. Moss's
two categories for writing assessment correspond roughly to the
divisions apparent in most testing companies in which content
personnel familiar with writing and its teaching work alongside
educational measurement specialists. I agree with Moss about
the isolation of college writing assessment from the educational
measurement community. In my own work, I have attempted to
bridge the gap between educational measurement and composition because, like Moss, I see the value in much work done in
educational measurement—not to mention the indebtedness of
all of us who work in writing assessment to the research carried
on for several decades that resulted in the development of
direct writing assessment. Unlike Moss, however, I see the isolation she refers to as existing on both sides. So, while college
writing assessment has been isolated from educational measurement, the converse is also true. Educational measurement has
been isolated not only from college writing assessment but from
the entire burgeoning field of composition.

To illustrate the isolation between educational assessment and
college English, I look at work that attempts to outline writing
assessment history, since historical inquiry can be a powerful
indicator of disciplinary allegiance and because, like this chapter,
histories tend to account for how a field came to be. In this sense,
we look to the past to understand why certain ideas, principles,
practices, theories and people are important to our present work.
Looking at the way certain scholars configure writing assessment
history is an indication not only of the values they hold as a individual members of a specific community but of the values of the
community itself. Writing assessment is a complex historical subject because it is an area that remains multidisciplinary, drawing

scholars and interest from across disciplines and fields. For my purposes, histories of writing assessment provide an interesting picture of the kinds of isolation or multidisciplinary interaction that create the current climate of the field. The next section, then, explores three different historical views of writing assessment. In these, I look for points of isolation and intersection not just to get a sense of the field as it now stands, but to be able to make some suggestions for the future state of the field with less isolation, more collaboration, and better assessments for teachers, students and all of those affected by writing assessment and its influence on teaching and learning.

Edward White has been the preeminent college composition scholar in writing assessment for three decades. His book, *Teaching and Assessing Writing*, published first in 1985 and in a second edition in 1994 (the edition I refer to throughout this volume) is easily the most popular source for information about writing assessment for college-level writing teachers and program administrators. Although White has never published a history of writing assessment, his retrospective essay "Holistic Scoring: Past Triumphs, Future Challenges" (1993) serves our purposes here by providing a description of the role holistic scoring and writing assessment have had on college-level writing instruction and program administration during the decades of the 1970s and 1980s.

White frames the early work he and others in the college writing community accomplished in the 1970s as a "missionary activity" (79). This missionary activity was in response to the prevalence of multiple choice tests for the measuring of writing ability at that time. According to White, he and others were involved in combat with ETS officials and college administrators to find more accurate and fair ways to assess student writing ability. Holistic scoring fit the needs of White and others, since it was a method for scoring student writing that "could come under the control of teachers" (79). White outlines the differences he sees in the way that holistic scoring sessions are run by testing companies like ETS and those that he and other English teachers administer: "It [ETS] tends to see too much debate about scores (or anything else) as time taken away from production of scores. But as campus and other faculty-run holistic scorings became more and more common, the warmth and fellowship they generated became one of their most valuable features" (88). Not only was holistic scoring a strong response to multiple choice tests, it also provided an important model for writing teachers themselves, since White claims that "When these same writing teachers returned to their classrooms [after holistic scoring sessions], they found that their teaching had changed. . . . [T]hey were able to use evaluation as a part of teaching, a great change from the customary empty whining about their responsibility for grading and testing" (89). The benefits of holistic scoring for teachers go beyond an attitude change toward assessment and provide them with models for assignment construction, fair grading practices, and the articulation of clear course goals.

White defines validity as "honesty and accuracy, with a demonstrated connection between what a test proclaims it is measuring and what it in fact measures" (90). He goes on to claim that holistic scoring is more valid than indirect measures. Most of White's discussion of validity has to do with ways in which holistic scoring might be less valid through shoddy task and prompt development and the inappropriate use of other testing procedures. His emphasis is on the technical features of the assessment itself. White's treatment of reliability is much more extensive than his discussion of validity; he devotes a little more than three pages to validity and almost seven to reliability. He acknowledges that "Reliability has been the underlying problem for holistic scoring since its origins" (93). White's conception of reliability, as I discuss in chapter four, is equated with fairness: "Reliability is a technical way of talking about simple fairness, and if we are not interested in fairness, we have no business giving tests or using test results" (93).

White's treatment of reliability underscores his belief that writing assessment is a site of contest and struggle. Ultimately, White's own position about reliability is ambiguous, as he ends his essay with a discussion of portfolios and reliability: "While reliability should not become the obsession for portfolio evaluation that it became for essay testing, portfolios cannot become a serious means of measurement without demonstrable reliability" (105). The contradictory impulses in White's essay are part of what I take as a love/hate relationship not only within White's notion of reliability, but evident even in the way that college English views writing assessment and the researchers who developed methods like holistic scoring. On the one hand, holistic scoring is seen as a powerful technique with the capability to effect "a minor revolution in a profession's approach to writing measurement and writing instruction" (79), while on the other hand, ETS is seen as a powerful force which must be resisted: "To this day, some of the ETS people involved do not understand why the community of writing teachers and writing researchers were—and are—so opposed to their socially and linguistically naïve work" (84). Interestingly enough, White refers only to ETS, ignoring any part that the educational measurement community might have had in developing direct writing assessment measures: "Aside from one book published by the College Board (Godshalk, Swineford & Coffman 1966) and a series of in-house documents at the Educational Testing Service, I found only material of questionable use and relevance in statistics and education" (81).

Kathleen Yancey's (1999) essay "Looking Back as We Look Forward: Historicizing Writing Assessment" appears in a commemorative issue of *College Composition and Communication* (*CCC*), celebrating the fiftieth volume of the journal, the main publication of the Conference on College Composition and Communication. Yancey's and White's notions of the field of writing assessment are through their understanding of composition studies. White begins his history of writing assessment in the early 1970s, around the time holistic scoring became an assessment option and around the same time rhetoric and composition began to come together as a field. Yancey begins her history in 1949, to coincide with the initial publication of *CCC*.

While White's narrative begins in the 1970s with English teachers awakening to the realities, challenges, and potential of getting involved in writing assessment. Yancey acknowledges assessment as an important but invisible part of writing instruction in the 1950s. For Yancey, writing assessment from 1950 onward can be seen as three consecutive waves: from 1950–1970, objective tests; from 1970–1986, holistically-scored essays; from 1986–present, portfolio assessment and programmatic assessment (483). Yancey sees the wave metaphor as a way to "historicize" the different "trends" in writing assessment: "with one wave feeding into another but without completely displacing the waves that came before" (483). Like White, Yancey sees the history of writing assessment as a struggle between teachers and testers: "the last fifty years of writing assessment can be narrativized as the teacher-layperson (often successfully) challenging the (psychometric) expert" (484).

Like White, Yancey sees the early layperson assessment pioneers as having a major role in the development of writing assessment procedures:

> Which is exactly what White and others—Richard Lloyd-Jones, Karen Greenberg, Lee Odell and Charles Cooper, to name a few—set out to do: devise a *writing* test that could meet the standard stipulated by the testing experts. . . . Administrators like White thus borrowed from the Advanced Placement Program at ETS their now familiar "testing technology." Called holistic writing assessment, the AP assessment, unlike the ETS-driven placement tests, was a classroom-implemented curriculum culminating in a final essay test that met adequate psychometric reliability standards. . . . By importing these procedures, test-makers like White could determine both what acceptable reliability for an essay test should be and, perhaps more important, how to get it. The AP testing technology, then, marks the second wave of writing assessment by making a more valid, classroom-like writing assessment possible. (490)

This version of how English teachers came to control and use holistic scoring is remarkably like the one offered by White.

One main difference is that White notes that ETS scoring sessions are fixated on the delivery of reliable scores whereas those run by him and other English teachers permit a more convivial and community-building atmosphere. Yancey, on the other hand, sees the main difference in that English teachers borrowed AP testing that is more closely allied to a specific curriculum, since AP testing (which ETS continues to conduct) is designed to measure how well high school students have mastered a specific course of study.

Another similarity between White's and Yancey's version of writing assessment history is that they both claim validity for direct writing assessment, and that their versions of validity "Validity means you are measuring what you intend to measure" (Yancey 487) are pretty much the same. However, instead of the contradictory impulses we see in White's attitude toward reliability, Yancey, notes that "Writing assessment is commonly understood as an exercise in balancing the twin concepts of validity and reliability" (487). Yancey goes on to suggest how the various waves she defines have affected the relationships between validity and reliability. In the first wave of "objective" tests, reliability was the main focus. In the second wave, validity became the focus. In the third wave, validity is increased because "if one text increases the validity of a test, how much more so two or three texts?" (491). She is careful to note the continuing role of reliability. Using Elbow and Belanoff's early work with portfolios at SUNY Stony Brook as a model, she contends that "psychometric reliability isn't entirely ignored" (492) as readers "are guided rather than directed by anchor papers and scoring guidelines" (493). In this way, I see Yancey as trying to talk about writing assessment in ways that are more amenable to the educational measurement community, since she attempts to characterize developments in college writing assessment in terms like reliability and validity that have their origins in, and continue to have important meaning for, the educational assessment community.

Despite Yancey's attempt, the picture both she and White paint of college writing assessment conforms to Moss's point about the mutual isolation between college writing assessment and educational measurement communities. In both accounts, English teachers are hero combatants who wrestle away control for writing assessment from testing companies who would ignore the need for writing assessment even to include any student writing. Whether we listen to White's version which has us see the faculty-run holistic scoring session as a virtual panacea for creating community, educating writing teachers, and producing accurate and fair scores for student writing, or to Yancey's, which distinguishes between "ETS-driven placement tests" (490) and holistic scoring developed for AP testing, the procedures under discussion were developed by the educational measurement community. And these procedures were basically identical, though I agree with White about the difference between an ETS scoring session and one run by English faculty. These test developers, like Fred Godshalk who coined the term "holistic scoring" in the early sixties, mostly worked for ETS. These are the people who experimented with training readers on scoring rubrics, so that independent readers would agree on scores at a rate that was psychometrically viable. This research culminated in the landmark study, conducted by Godshalk, Swineford and Coffman (1966) and published as a research bulletin by ETS in 1966, in which independent readers were finally able to score student writing at an acceptable rate of reliability. The procedures used in this study, like rater training on numerical scoring rubrics became the technology of direct writing assessment that continues to be used today. The educational measurement community created direct writing assessment as they had created the indirect tests. While pioneers in writing assessment outside the educational measurement community like Edward White (1994), Charles Cooper (1977) and Richard Lloyd-Jones (1977) struggled to implement the new procedures in a variety of situations and to bring them under English faculty control, the procedures themselves were created by educational measurement specialists working for ETS to provide a reliable way to score student writing.

Unlike White (1994), Yancey (1999) attempts to portray developments in writing assessment through the concepts of validity and reliability, with reliability being the main focus of indirect tests, and validity being the focus of direct writing assessments, like holistic scoring. Yancey contends that validity "dominated the second wave of writing assessment" (489) which Yancey pinpoints as the holistically scored essay during the time period between 1970 and 1986. However, Yancey's contention is not supported by the literature on writing assessment. While working on my dissertation in the fall of 1986, I conducted a complete Educational Research Information Clearinghouse (ERIC) search and found 156 listings for writing assessment in the entire database. Of these, over sixty percent were devoted to reliability. It was clear to me then, and it's clear to me now, that reliability dominated scholarship on writing assessment during that time period. I can think of two reasons why Yancey mistakes the 1970–1986 time period in writing assessment as being dominated by concerns for validity. One might be that she, like White, sees holistic scoring and other direct writing assessment procedures as a victory (coded as validity) won by English teachers over the educational measurement community (coded as reliability). Therefore in her mind, the proliferation of holistic scoring[1] allowed validity to dominate. A second reason might be that, because of her disciplinary affiliation, she is isolated from the scholarship on reliability and its connection to holistic scoring and other direct writing assessment procedures. The struggle that resulted in the development of holistic scoring took place within the field of educational measurement, since both indirect and traditional direct writing assessment were developed and designed to address problems in reliability caused by independently scored essays.

One of the biggest points of isolation between college writing assessment and educational measurement is in the treatment of validity. Both White and Yancey posit the outmoded definition of validity as a test that measures what it purports to measure. This impoverished definition allows for claims of validity regardless of the theoretical orientation of the assessment or its consequences. For example, the recent writing assessment used by City University of New York can be pronounced valid, since the consequences of denying university entrance to scores of minority students does not interfere with what the test purports to measure. The test continues to be used to deny educational opportunities to students even though there is a body of evidence that shows that students who worked in developmental and mainstream programs were able to pass "the core courses at a rate that was even higher than the rate for our pilot course students who had placed into English 110" (Gleason 2000, 568). As I note throughout the volume and expand later in this discussion, validity has for decades meant more than whether an assessment measures what it purports to measure. Currently, validity focuses on the adequacy of the theoretical and empirical evidence to construct an argument for making decisions based upon a specific assessment. In contrast to the picture of validity offered by White and Yancey, over thirty years ago the educational community had already established an alternative concept of validity: "One validates not a test but the interpretation of data arising from a specific procedure" (Cronbach 1971, 447). White and Yancey assume the validity of direct writing assessment, with Yancey attributing increases in validity to assessments that are more "classroom-like" (490) or that contain multiple texts (491). Unfortunately, the validity of holistic scoring, the most popular form of direct writing assessment, has been asserted but never established—a point made by Davida Charney (1984) nearly two decades ago and seconded by me a few years later (Huot 1990). Whether or not validity as a guiding principle for assessment is something writing assessment should pursue is a separate issue and one I address later in this chapter. Nonetheless, it is clear from the two pieces by White and Yancey that college writing assessment has held a very different version of validity from that currently advocated by those in educational measurement.

Our somewhat cursory examination of scholarship from college writing assessment reveals, as Moss indicates, its isolation from educational measurement. However, the converse is also true. Work on writing assessment from educational measurement exhibits an isolation from college writing assessment. To illustrate the isolation of educational measurement from college writing assessment, I choose to look at Roberta Camp's (1993) essay, "Changing the Model for the Direct Assessment of Writing" which was first published in an anthology I edited with Michael Williamson; a briefer version was published three years later in an anthology edited by Edward White, William Lutz and Sandra Kamuskiri. Camp is a well-known figure in writing assessment, working for ETS through most of her professional career. Her early work on portfolios was influential in making them such a popular writing assessment option. This essay, while not strictly a history of writing assessment, suits our purposes well as Camp outlines in the beginning, "The discussion will begin with a reflection on the history of writing assessment in recent decades and then go on to examine the current status of existing models for writing assessment" (46).

Like Yancey, Camp sees writing assessment history as balancing the requirements of reliability and validity. She explains how multiple choice tests of writing ability measure writing and how these tests claim validity.

> The multiple choice test, with its machine-scoreable items, provides evidence taken from multiple data points representing relatively discrete components of the writing task each measured separately . . . The claims for its validity have rested on its coverage of skills necessary to writing and on correlations between test scores and course grades—or more recently between test scores and performance on samples of writing, including writing generated under classroom conditions. (47)

Camp notes that these claims for the validity of multiple choice tests of writing were more persuasive "to statistically oriented members of the measurement community than to teachers of writing" (47). While Camp is ultimately sympathetic to those who would question the use of multiple choice tests, she does note that there is some foundation for the validity claims of indirect measures of writing. Camp explains that eventually research indicated that although student scores on multiple choice tests and essay exams would be similar, that these "formats," as Camp calls them, were ultimately measuring different "skills."

Although Camp is a proponent of direct writing assessment, she is guarded in her claims for its validity: "In many respects, the holistically scored writing sample fares better than the multiple choice test with respect to validity . . . It has therefore been seen by some writing assessment practitioners as a stand-alone format for more valid assessment, especially when more than one writing sample is used" (49). For Camp, "the estimated test reliability for a single essay scored twice is insufficient to fully justify the use of a single essay as the sole basis for important judgments about students' academic careers" (49). The solution to this problem with the reliability of holistically scored essays is, in Camp's terms, a "compromise" which entails using both multiple choice tests and holistically scored essays. Camp acknowledges the importance of direct writing assessment and the many advances that have been made in the ways "we conduct evaluation sessions and report the results" (51).

In reflecting upon the history of writing assessment, Camp also attempts to look at the assumptions behind the procedures. She contends that many of the procedures designed to make writing assessment reliable might contribute to a questioning of its validity, since the streamlined process of having students write to identical prompts in test-like conditions only represents a portion of what we consider to be the skill of writing. This is in contrast to her assertion that a single-scored essay lacks the reliability to be valid. Camp refers to literature about the complexities of reading and writing that have emerged in recent years and concludes that both multiple choice tests and impromptu essays are lacking in their ability to measure the complexity involved in writing: "Neither the multiple-choice test nor the impromptu writing sample provides a basis in the assessment for obtaining information about the metacognitive aspects of writing, information that is essential to instruction and the writer's development" (58). Camp contends that the more traditional forms of writing assessment are inadequate given the many recent breakthroughs in research, theory and practice about written communication: "The multiple choice test and the writing sample seem clearly insufficient for measuring writing ability as we now understand it" (58). For Camp, advances in knowledge about reading and writing have fueled advances in the assessment of student writing. Camp advocates that "we need to develop a conceptual framework for writing assessment that reflects our current understanding of writing" (59).

Camp contends that "the recent developments in cognitive psychology that have stimulated new perspectives on writing have brought new views of intellectual behavior and learning to all of education, including the field of assessment" (60). She focuses on changes in validity which no longer rest on the coverage of an assessment and comparisons to performances by students with other measures—the methodology implemented to justify the use of multiple-choice tests for measuring student writing. Instead, Camp asserts "that all evidence for validity is to be interpreted in relation to the theoretical construct, the purpose for the assessment, and therefore the inferences derived from it, and the social consequences" (61). The question for validity is no longer just whether or not a test measures what it purports to measure but rather "whether our assessments adequately represent writing as we understand it" (61).

Camp urges the creation of new models for writing assessment that capitalize on the continuing development of more complex understandings of literacy and its teaching. Combining a theory of learning which is emerging from cognitive psychology with recent developments in validity should allow us to create assessments for writing "that lead far beyond the narrow focus on score reliability and the constricted definitions of validity that characterized earlier discussions of the measurement properties of writing assessments" (68). Focusing on research about the composing process and building upon the lessons we have learned through the use of direct writing assessment should provide a productive future for writing assessment and the creation of new, alternative models. She outlines three stages for the development of these models that focus on, first, identifying the competencies to be assessed and specifications for "the tasks to be presented" (69), second, "exploring scoring systems, and further refining tasks and scoring systems" (69), and third, "training readers" (69), "scoring samples," (69) and "conducting statistical and qualitative analyses to establish reliability, validity and generalizability" (69). Camp contends that "Procedures such as these suggest an orderly and responsible approach to developing and trying out new assessments of writing" (69).

Camp ends her chapter by pointing out that writing assessments are often lauded in educational measurement circles as being "exemplary as models for assessment" (70), since they attempt to represent and model the complexities of literate behavior. In characterizing what she sees as the future of writing assessment, Camp forecasts several features that have to do with creating an increased context within which student writers can work and in providing assessment activities and results that are more meaningful to teachers' professional development and understanding of their students' abilities. She also notes an increased attention and awareness of the cognitive processes involved in writing.

If, in college writing assessment history, English teachers are combatants in a struggle to wrest away control of writing assessment from testing experts, they are non-players in the historical accounting from educational measurement. They might have concern for including writing in its assessment (47), and, like White, Camp thinks that "No responsible educator would want to see a return to evaluations of writing based on the private idiosyncrasies of the individual evaluator" (58), but in Camp's history they otherwise have no role in writing assessment. Ignoring the role of early college writing assessment pioneers in this way not only dismisses their contributions but it also misses the development of a culture and advocacy that would eventually clamor for assessments more compatible with writing instruction, and that eventually lead to portfolios (Elbow and Belanoff 1986) and writing assessments that go beyond the psychometric paradigm (Allen 1995; Haswell and Wyche-Smith 1994; Smith 1993).

For Camp, writing assessment has consisted of a "compromise" between multiple-choice tests and holistically scored essays. Camp even admits that holistically scored essays neither represent the complexity of writing nor do they, by themselves, satisfy the measurement requirements for reliability. Given this description of holistic scoring, I have to wonder exactly who or what is being compromised? We have multiple choice tests of usage and grammar that involve no writing or reading at all (though Camp contends that they do sample relevant content-area knowledge), and holistic scoring that according to Camp under-represents the process of writing while at the same failing to achieve necessary reliability. Unfortunately, I and others in college writing assessment would see no compromise here, but rather a continuing, unrelenting march toward reliability at the expense of validity—and complete dismissal of those outside educational measurement.

A continuing theme throughout this chapter is Camps's assertion that writing assessments began to change as our understanding of the complexity of writing became more apparent. This is a progressive agenda for writing assessment development that is driven by the knowledge we have about writing itself. It is also a view in which the responsibility for the problematic assessments of the past rest with content-area professionals, since once content-area professionals began to supply a more accurate and complex picture of the act of writing, assessments were developed to match. However, Camp offers no evidence for this assertion; she merely correlates advancements in writing assessment with those in literacy studies. Her position ignores the theoretical entrenchment of many in the educational measurement community. And, as I argue in chapter four, it is the beliefs and assumptions behind theoretical and epistemological positions that drive writing assessment practice. For example, as late as

1984, her colleague at ETS, Peter Cooper, writes, "From a psychometric point of view, it does appear that indirect assessment alone can afford a satisfactory measure of writing skills for ranking and selection purposes" (27). Keep in mind that this publication date is after many of the landmark studies on the writing process which Camp cites as being influential in promoting the development of new writing assessments. Even as late as 1998, Roger Cherry and Steven Witte write about the under-representation of writing in most assessments. Camp's assertion about the preeminent role of content knowledge about writing and literacy is an interesting and important idea that I hope guides writing assessment in the future, since it positions content-area knowledge in a leadership role. Currently, however, content-area professionals in testing corporations play a subordinate role; theories of testing—and not of language—drive most current writing assessments (see chapter four for a discussion of the theories that drive current traditional writing assessment).

Ironically, Camp does not mention assessments developed upon theories of language rather than testing (Allen 1995; Haswell and Wyche-Smith 1994; Lowe and Huot 1997; Smith 1993). While this work appears in print after or concurrent with the publication of this essay in 1993, Camp's second version of this essay in 1996 contains no references to this work. For me, Camp's neglect of work in assessment that calls for the very principles she advocates is due to her isolation from the college writing assessment community. This isolation can also be seen in the absence in her discussion of the influence of composition as a burgeoning field during the last three decades in which the direct assessment of writing has been evolving. Not only does Camp's isolation prevent her from tapping into new developments in writing assessment, but it also causes her to miss much of the new emphasis in language and literacy studies on the social nature of literate behavior (Berlin 1988; Bizzell 1992; Faigley 1992; and many others). Instead, Camp refers repeatedly to the advances in cognitive studies about the complexities of the way students write and learn. Her isolation from college writing assessment, then, causes her to miss the development of new, language-based writing assessments and the continuing appreciation of the social aspects of literacy and its teaching, which have been a continuing focus in the composition literature since the mid-1980s.

This review is necessarily brief and incomplete, but it nonetheless shows how college English writing assessment professionals and educational measurement professionals—the two major communities responsible for the ongoing development of writing assessment—have been isolated from each other. Neither community has given the other the credit or respect for its accomplishments and contributions. We fail to recognize the debts we have to each other or the ways in which work in one area is stunted by its isolation from the other. While English teachers who work in assessment have often portrayed researchers in educational measurement as the bad guys (Elbow 1996; White 1994), more recent work from educational measurement refers to the efforts of English teachers as unreasonable and naive (Breland 1996; Scharton 1996).

VALIDITY

I began this chapter by noting that the work being done in writing assessment is constrained, shaped and promoted by the overall shape of the field itself. Tracing the two main influences on writing assessment, it is easy to see how both college writing assessment and educational measurement have been the prime shapers of what we know as writing assessment theory, research and practice. My examination of the way writing assessment history is represented by those in college writing assessment and educational measurement reveals two different versions of the field itself. As my discussion of the two historical representations indicates, both sides of the assessment coin are partial and limited; neither provides a complete enough picture of the complexities, issues and resources necessary to move writing assessment forward as a field of study. The isolation that Moss (1998) notes not only hinders any work undertaken in either side of the field but, I believe, limits the field itself. I am not advocating a quick and dirty effort, by which writing assessment simply combines approaches from the two fields; there are conflicts and tensions that hardly fit together. White (1994) and others have already suggested a stakeholder approach that attempts to address the disparate concerns of people working in different fields for the assessment of student writing. What we need are some new directions for writing assessment scholarship, and practices that involve and attract both factions interested and invested in writing assessment. I hope to provide a framework that will make it possible for all those who work in writing to create new ways of theorizing and practicing assessment. While I outline this framework here, I write also in chapters four, six, and seven about the importance of validity theory in directing writing assessment toward a stronger role in promoting teaching and learning.

I begin this discussion of how we might create a new framework for writing assessment with a discussion of validity. Both sides of the writing assessment community talk about validity, though they talk about it different ways. The first step, then, is to take a closer look at validity. Although I see validity as an important part of all writing assessment, it cannot by itself mend the isolation in the field or provide a productive future for writing assessment. But it can perhaps provide a unifying focus that permits those in different fields to bridge gaps and make connections. It is possible that validity can be a way to make all those who work in writing assessment responsible to a given set of principles. Of course, it might be said that this has always been validity's role and that given the discussion of the field so far, it has failed, since we cannot at this juncture in writing assessment even agree upon what validity is, let alone agree to abide by its principles. There are two principles, however, that might enable us to use validity as a linchpin for holding together writing assessment, preventing the current isolation of those who now work in the area and charting a productive future. First of all, we need to agree on what validity is—to decide what the principles for working in writing assessment should be. Secondly, we must hold each other responsible for following these principles. Although validity theory has been developed within the educational measurement community, that community has not always worked within the theoretical framework it provides (Shepard, 1993).

Both White (1994) and Yancey (1999) define validity as making sure a test measures what it purports to measure, though neither of them cite any source for this. This textbook definition can be found in many discussions about validity, but such a definition by itself is inadequate for many reasons. As Yancey notes in using the definition and citing F. Alan Hanson's book (1993) *Testing Testing: The Social Consequences of an Examined Life,* an assessment can create the categories for which it assesses. For example, I could use holistic scoring to make decisions about which students at the University of Louisville, where I work, have adequate writing skills to exit the first-year composition sequence. We could claim that the test measures what it purports to measure, since it would involve students writing and teachers reading that writing. We could cite adequate levels of interrater reliability, a scoring rubric that is general enough not to evoke any argument about its descriptions of writing ability, and the other trappings associated with holistic scoring, and eventually that test would come to represent writing ability in the first-year composition sequence at the University of Louisville. Instructors would begin including instruction on passing the test as a part of their curricula, so that their students would be successful on the test and even more importantly would be deemed good writers. Eventually, this test of writing would be the marker of good writing, de facto a valid test. All of this would take place without any attention to the decisions being made on the basis of this assessment. The assessment would exist outside of any determination about its impact on the writing, education, or lives of the students required to take the test, not to mention the test's impact on the curriculum of the course that students take before being tested. This example points out that such a limited definition of validity is not only inadequate, it is dangerous because it accords an unexamined authority to an assessment that has the power to define educational achievement and influence instruction. My make-believe scenario closely resembles the real-life example of the ways in which the CUNY placement test is used to deny entry to many students (Gleason, 2000), underscoring the problematic nature of any form of validity that does not consider the consequences of the decisions made on the results of an assessment.

Since the 1950s, validity has been defined in more complex and comprehensive ways that attempt to provide more and more information not only about the test itself, but also about the theoretical framework that supports specific testing practices and the consequences on students and schools that result from the decisions made on the basis of the test. Before the 1950s, a more simple and reductionist notion of validity prevailed. For example, in 1946, J. P. Guilford states that "a test is valid for anything with which it correlates" (429). This notion of validity resting on a correlation to an outside criterion eventually became known as criterion validity. As validity theory developed, criterion became one of three forms of validity about which Robert Guion (1980) coined the term "the holy trinity." Criterion validity refers to the relationship of a measure to outside and relevant criteria. The second form of validity was content validity which pertained to the domain of knowledge, ability, or trait being measured. The third form of validity was called construct validity, and referred to the construct of the ability, skill, or performance being measured. For example, in writing assessment, the question would be whether or not the assessment contained an adequate construct of writing ability.

While certainly more complex than earlier definitions of validity, the trinitarian notion of validity had other shortcomings. Although content, criterion, and construct validity were never meant to function independently of each other, they were often reified and used independently, so that test developers could assert validity for a measure even if it were only a partial claim based upon content or criterion validity. For example, as Camp (1993) details, multiple choice tests of grammar and mechanics based their claim for validity on both content and criterion validity. It was asserted that testing students on grammar and mechanics (later indirect tests even added questions about the writing process or rhetorical decision-making) sampled relevant content-area knowledge. Claims based on criterion validity noted that student scores on multiple choice tests correlated to some extent with the scores these same students received on essays they had written. Consequently, validity was asserted for multiple choice testing of an ability (writing) without there being any writing in the assessment itself. Of course, had the test developers considered construct validity, no such claim would have been possible.

Eventually, measurement scholars and validity theorists proposed a unified version of validity under the construct validity framework within which considerations of content and criterion would be subsumed. The intent of formulating validity as a unitary concept was to prohibit the parceling out of validity piecemeal to allow partial claims for the validity of an assessment. In other words, even though a multiple choice test could claim that it sampled relevant content from the writing process or that scores on the test had certain levels of correlation with scores on essay exams, a claim for validity would have to contain evidence that the exam represented a viable construct of the act of writing—a most difficult claim for a writing test that contains no writing.

Validity as a concept, then, has evolved from a simple correlation to "an integrated evaluative judgment of the degree to which empirical evidence and theoretical rationales support the adequacy and appropriateness of inferences and actions based on test scores or other modes of assessment" (Messick 1989a, 5). Messick's definition is widely cited and accepted in the educational measurement community. I use it, then, as a way to understand how his definition of validity contrasts with the one currently used by the college writing assessment community and to emphasize how Messick's notion of validity can be applied to writing assessment. One of the biggest differences between Messick's version of validity and that commonly used in college writing assessment is the amount of information and activity necessary to satisfy a claim for validity. Instead of just looking at whether or not an assessment measures what it's supposed to, Messick's definition requires that we collect empirical evidence and furnish a theoretical rationale. Validity centers not on the measurement itself but on the "adequacy" of the decisions and "actions" that are taken based on the assessment. In this way, validity cannot be seen as a singular blanket that covers any assessment procedure like holistic scoring or portfolios. Information about decisions to be made and actions to be taken need to be supplied for each use of the assessment, negating not only a simple declaration of validity for a specific type of assessment, but introducing the necessity of supplying empirical and theoretical evidence of validity for specific environments, populations and curricula. In this way, validity supports the local and site-based assessment practices I discuss in chapter four, since "validity must be established for each particular use of a test" (Shephard 1993, 406).

In answering the question "What does it mean to say that actions based on test scores must be supported by evidence?" Lorrie Shephard (1993 406) uses the example of school readiness testing whose results are used to make some kindergartners wait a year before beginning their formal education. Shephard claims that in order to be valid, these decisions should be based upon evidence, showing that children profit from sitting out an extra year. In fact, no such evidence exists, with comparative studies even "show[ing] no academic benefit and some emotional harm" (407). This example about validity and readiness testing has strong implications for writing assessment, whether we refer to my earlier example of the placement testing at CUNY upon which the decision was made to deny entrance to certain students, or to the placement testing common at many colleges and universities that requires some students to take remedial courses before they can enroll in regular, credit-bearing writing courses. In order to supply sufficient evidence about the validity of writing placement programs, we need to know how well those students denied entrance to a certain institution, or placed in a remedial class, ended up doing as a result of the decision that was based upon our placement procedures. Much more information is needed than is currently supplied by those who would consider our writing placement programs "valid."

In addition to requiring more evidence for claims of validity, there are additional differences between the way that college writing assessment has defined and talked about validity and the ways in which validity has been used by the educational assessment measurement community to make validity claims for its writing assessments. In either case, validity as it has been theorized is not the same as the practice used by either camp in writing assessment to justify the use of its assessments. I think it's possible and potentially very beneficial to view validity not as some pronouncement of approval but rather as an ongoing process of critical reflection (Moss 1998). In this way, as Moss and others (Bourdieu and Wacquant 1992; Cherryholmes 1988) advocate, validity is a way that "the inquiry lens is turned back on researchers and program developers themselves as stakeholders, encouraging critical reflection about their own theories and practices" (Moss 1998, 119).

CREATING A FIELD FOR WRITING ASSESSMENT

There is much to be gained for both the college writing assessment community and the educational measurement community if they would begin to use validity together as a way not only of regulating themselves and their assessments but also of developing assessments upon which decisions about writing can best be made. We have seen throughout this chapter that the isolation and conflict in writing assessment has been characterized in different ways, depending upon who tells the story. Probably the tension between the two camps in writing assessment can best be summarized as a conflict between values, between the need to produce consistent and replicable scores in an efficient manner and the need to represent the complexity and variety inherent in written communication. A few years ago, I was part of a group helping to develop the writing test for the National Assessment of Educational Progress (NAEP). Our group was made up primarily of people who either worked in college writing assessment or were otherwise connected to the teaching of English. At one of the first meetings, we were being introduced to the new NAEP writing assessment by the psychometrician who was overseeing the project. He told us the parameters for the writing portion of NAEP, and how the budget was tighter than for the last writing assessment, and that even though he saw real value in projects like the 1992 portfolio portion of the previous writing assessment, this time, there just wouldn't be the resources for bells and whistles; he said that they were hoping for mostly single-sample twenty minute essays. Most of us who worked in English rather than measurement were a little stunned. However, James Marshall, who teaches in the School of Education at the University of Iowa put it best. "Your bells and whistles," he said "are our meat and potatoes." Much of the work we did as a group over an eighteen-month period could probably be characterized as trying to explain how what the educational measurement community considered to be fringe or extra accessories was for the English teaching community the heart of assessing student writing. In this situation, as in most of writing assessment conducted outside of the college writing community, the measurement people were clearly in charge, and most of the NAEP writing assessment went off as it had been initially planned by the personnel overseeing the project, regardless of much feedback to the contrary.

Including theoretical input about the complexity and context necessary to adequately represent written communication as a part of the validity process gives writing teachers and writing program administrators a real say about not only the ways in which student writing is assessed, but also the ways it is defined and valued. Of course, this does not mean that validity is an easy way for college writing assessment to take over writing assessment as a field of study. While it allows the English teaching community a greater say in writing assessment, it also imparts other responsibilities. Validity inquiry requires what the educational measurement community calls "rival hypothesis testing," a process in which alternative explanations from both theoretical and empirical sources must be offered as well as alternative decisions based on the evidence. This consideration of rival explanations and actions is a central part of validity: "any validation effort still consists of stating hypotheses and challenging them by seeking evidence to the contrary" (Shephard 417). The process of considering rival explanations and actions is probably a sound method for any kind of serious thought. In writing assessment, however, it might be particularly crucial because it is a field in which, as we have seen, two competing communities are ready to advance different explanations for existing phenomena and different ways of gathering information to make important decisions about literacy education. Any validity inquiry in writing assessment, then, needs to include a serious consideration of rival theories, methods, explanations and actions, so that it includes a consideration of the values, ideas and explanations possible from both camps.

Lee Cronbach, a major figure in validity theory, characterizes validity and the act of validation as argument: "Validation speaks to a diverse and potentially critical audience; therefore, the argument must link concepts, evidence, social and personal consequences and values" (1988, 4). Two things make Cronbach's notion of validity as argument especially pertinent to writing assessment. One, his idea that validation documentation and research needs to speak to "a diverse and potentially critical audience" could not be more true considering our discussion of the two major camps in writing assessment. His point also highlights the necessity of building validity arguments that speak not only to those who share our disciplinary allegiances and theoretical and epistemological orientations, but to those who don't, as well. This imperative to use validity to cross disciplinary boundaries is crucial if we are going to work against the isolation between college writing assessment and educational measurement and create a real field for the theory and practice of writing assessment.

The concept of the stakeholder is common in educational measurement, and it has been used by some in college writing assessment (White 1994), as we discussed earlier, to note the various kinds of people with an interest in writing assessment and the positions they hold. Conceiving of validity as a way to convince those who do not hold similar positions seems a significant way to account for difference in writing assessment. Using rival-hypothesis testing can make our arguments more palpable for a wide range of audiences. I see this concept in constructing validity arguments as way to work against a notion of writing assessment as dominated by distinct stakeholders with claims for varying degrees of attention to different theories and practices.

Trying to construct writing assessments that honor the legitimate claims of various stakeholders can result not only in the missed opportunity to create an assessment that can enhance teaching and learning, but it can also build assessments that are ultimately failures. The notion of honoring stakeholder's claims also ignores the politics of power. All stakeholders are not equal, and all claims will not and practically speaking cannot be equally honored. The need for technical specifications (Breland 1996; Camp 1996; Koretz 1993; Scharton 1996) or political control (Huot and Williamsom 1997) is often seen as more important than theoretical knowledge from the content area (Cherry and Witte 1998) or the needs and concerns of teachers (Callahan 1997, 1999) and students (Moss 1996; Spaulding and Cummings 1998). In writing assessment, the results of this unequal power struggle have been practices which score portfolios paper by paper to achieve interrater reliability (Nystrand, Cohen, and Dowling 1993) or portfolio systems that please neither the teachers (Callahan 1997, 1999), the students (Spaulding and Cummings 1998), school administrators, or politicians. Instead of attempting to honor disparate claims of unequal influence, we need to build writing assessment practices that have a firm content-area theoretical basis and the potential to enhance teaching and learning. Emphasizing that validity addresses the decisions made on behalf of an assessment can only increase the importance of stakeholders like teachers, their immediate supervisors and students themselves, since it is these people who are most knowledgeable about the local educational process. Privileging the roles of teachers and students makes sure that assessment does not overshadow educational concerns.

In considering testing company personnel, I emphasize the role of content-area specialists like teachers and scholars from the supporting disciplines because their concerns are not usually considered in most large-scale or high stakes assessments. I also emphasize the role of content-area personnel in writing assessment because educational measurement specialists with no credentials in writing, rhetoric, linguistics or language education are not the best equipped people to integrate pedagogical implications in a writing assessment. Writing assessment as a contested intellectual site is an anomaly in educational measurement, since most other content-area fields do not have an active role in their assessments. Although I think it important to give additional power and responsibility to content-area professionals in writing, this responsibility also includes the necessity of constructing strong validity arguments. Any use of any writing assessment should be accompanied with a validity argument that addresses technical documentation important to those who work in educational measurement, honors political considerations important to administrative and governmental agencies, and most importantly considers the impact on the educational environment and the consequences for individual students and teachers. If validity arguments that consider all possible explanations and evidence are constructed, then those with various positions in a writing assessment can be represented. However, given that the commitment of validity theorists like Cronbach (1988), Messick (1989a, 1989b), Moss (1992), and Shephard (1993) clearly outlines the importance of assessment in creating environments conducive to teaching and learning, it follows that if we are committed to assessments that promote teaching and learning, then we must listen primarily to the voice of educators and their students.

The second important aspect of Cronbach's characterization of validity as argument is that many of those in college writing assessment have a specific connection to the study of argument, since rhetorical study is an important resource for the field of composition. Not only does validity as argument pose more of an interest to those with a strong sense of rhetoric, it also give them a rhetorical heuristic for learning to construct validity arguments that contain a strong consideration of alternate views as well as an understanding of how to create arguments that are compelling to various audiences. Validity as argument provides the possibility for people who work in English departments and teach writing but are isolated from the literature and discipline of educational measurement to see validity as something familiar, understandable and valuable. White (1994a) has urged those interested in or responsible for writing assessment to become more knowledgeable about statistics and technical testing concepts like reliability, while at the same time promoting too simplistic an understanding of validity. I contend that college writing assessment and English teachers are better served by a current knowledge of validity theory. Validity in its rhetorical sense provides a way for college writing assessment to connect its assessment theories, scholarship, literature and practices to those in educational measurement. Of course, part of the rhetorical assignment college writing assessment developers undertake is to learn more about what the audience of those in educational measurement value if they are to be able to write validity arguments that convince educational measurement scholars. If we can promote the regular use of validity arguments that attempt to be compelling for all of those who work in writing assessment, then it might be possible to ease the current climate of isolation, since both camps in writing assessment would need to know about each other in order to make convincing arguments for validity.

In concluding this chapter, I hope to able to outline some new ways in which writing assessment can be understood as a field of study. It is clear that so far, writing assessment has been carried out by two different groups of scholars with different theoretical, epistemological and disciplinary orientations. Neither of the two camps has understood that the other is capable of enriching not only both points of view but writing assessment as a whole. In minimizing each other's contributions to writing assessment, each group has advanced its own impoverished version of writing assessment theory and practice. There are legitimate arguments from each side. College writing assessment can claim that the educational measurement community has advanced assessments that are not only ignorant of the ways in which people learn to read and write, but that these assessments have had deleterious effects on individual students and whole writing programs. Educational measurement can claim that college writing assessment not only appropriated measurement concepts, techniques and practices without acknowledging their origins but even ultimately misused them.

Validity, in its broadest and most current sense, can be a rallying point for both college writing assessment and educational measurement. Validity that looks not just at technical and statistical explanations but that focuses on the decisions and the consequences of those decisions made on behalf of an assessment cannot but help to appeal to those in college writing assessment. Validity as we have been discussing it and as the literature in educational measurement has been detailing for the last three decades has much to recommend it to the college writing assessment community. Stipulating that all claims for validity must consider theoretical and empirical evidence provides an opportunity for college writing assessment specialists to become full partners with their educational measurement counterparts. As I discuss in chapter six, reconceptualizing writing assessment as research rather than as a technical apparatus provides new leadership roles for teachers and administrators. Validity also imparts new responsibilities for college writing assessment,

since even if a department decides to use commercially prepared writing assessments, it is their obligation to provide a
validity argument for each use of a test. Conversely, educational
measurement scholars must begin to recognize the site-based,
locally controlled assessments that are now being developed at
many institutions. What I hope is that not only will those in educational measurement begin to recognize these assessments but
that they will begin to help those in college writing assessment
improve them and the validity arguments constructed for
them.[2] Clearly, no matter which version of the field we sub-
scribe to, there is much work to be done in writing assessment,
and to accomplish this work, we need to draw on all the
resources we have at our disposal. Creating a field of writing
assessment that promotes communication, dialogue and debate
can only increase our knowledge and understanding and
improve the assessments we can create.

3

ASSESSING, GRADING, TESTING, AND TEACHING WRITING

As Kathleen Yancey (1999) points out in her history of writing assessment, evaluation in some form or another has been an important part of college writing courses for over fifty years. Yancey's history recognizes the often conflicted nature of assessment for the teaching of writing. Although most writing teachers recognize the importance and necessity of regular assessment, they are also rightly concerned about the adverse effects that assessment can have on their classrooms and students. This chapter focuses on the kind of assessment that takes place within a classroom context; it looks at assessing, grading and testing writing, since when we talk about classroom assessment, we also speak of grades and tests, at times using all three terms interchangeably. This slippage of assessment, grading and testing toward interchangeability promotes an attitude about assessment that is often critical and unexamined.

The result of the strong connections between grading, testing and assessing writing is that any possible connection between the teaching and evaluating of student writing is seldom questioned or discussed. In chapter two, I noted the negative attitude toward assessment in an introduction to a special issue of *English Journal*, the NCTE journal for high school English teachers. The very focus on assessment came with a disclaimer and an apologetic tone. In chapter six, we'll see John Stalnaker, then head of the College Board, berate English teachers for their beliefs and assumptions about writing assessment. These kinds of attitudes from both teachers and testers have led those who teach writing to believe that assessing student writing somehow interferes with their ability to teach it. There are of course, some notable exceptions. For example, Edward White's germinal text is called *Teaching and Assessing Writing* (1994), and he includes the ways formal assessments like holistic scoring can benefit classroom practice. But even White divides assessment and teaching into separate entities that can affect each other. Certainly portfolios have been constructed by some (Elbow 1991; Camp and Levine 1991) as ways to link assessment and teaching, but they have also been constructed as better off without any evaluative element at all (Hamilton 1994; Sunstein 1996).

Even in our consideration of how students assess themselves, we have focused primarily on the ways in which one's progress in writing is connected to one's grades or success in school. The ability of students to assess themselves has long been an important pedagogical (Beaven 1977; Marting 1991; and others) and research (Beach 1976; Beach and Eaton 1984; and others) concern in composition. In fact, the reflective writing often included in portfolios has also been seen as an important tool for student self-assessment (Armstrong 1991; Mills-Courts and Amiran 1991; Yancey 1998). While self-assessment is certainly an important ability for the developing writer and is related to a student's ability to use assessment to write (Smith and Yancey 2000), it is often focused on how well students measure their progress in a particular class (Beaven 1977) or on how well or how much they have revised (Beach 1976; Beach and Eaton 1984). There is a limited amount of research on how students and other writers evaluate writing. Thomas Hilgers reports on two studies (1984; 1986) of children, grades two through six, and their ability to evaluate writing quality. In both studies, Hilgers notes that the ability to assess writing is related to the ability to write, and that it appears at those early ages to be part of a developmental process. Susan Miller (1982) found through interviews and surveys of college-age and professional writers that most writers did not want to evaluate themselves. Student writers were most influenced by teacher evaluations; on the other hand, the majority of professional writers reported not being influenced by others. More recently Richard Larson (2000) writes about the connection of assessment to the ability to revise one's prose. Ellen Schendel and Peggy O'Neill (1999) write about the possible problems associated with self-assessment and the need for a more critical understanding of some of the assumptions behind self assessment practices in writing assessment.

These writer attitudes point to the fact that we have evolved pedagogies that conceive of teaching as a coaching and enabling process, while holding onto conceptions of evaluation as a means for gate-keeping and upholding standards. Assessment practices that use grades and teachers' written comments as ways to "sort" students or demand mastery of certain "skills" outside the context of a specific piece of writing remain at odds with a pedagogy that recognizes students' socially positioned nature as language users. These practices ultimately deny that linguistic, rhetorical and literate capabilities can only be developed within the context of discovering and making meaning with the written word. We have yet to create in any substantive way a pedagogy that links the teaching and assessing of writing.

GRADING, TESTING AND ASSESSING

In this chapter, I propose to examine in some detail what we mean by grading, testing and assessing student writing and to use the analysis to suggest alternative practices that recast assessment's role in the writing classroom. I hope to unpack the beliefs and assumptions that support these practices in order to bring to light the often unexamined and untheorized ideas that inform our current assessment practices; for only if we examine and interrogate our underlying theoretical positions can we ever hope to alter classroom practice in any substantive way. Two main assumptions about assessment and the teaching of writing undergird my approach. One assumption is that in literate activity, assessment is everywhere. No matter what purpose we have for the reading and writing we do, we evaluate what we read and write on a fairly continuous basis. The second assumption is that being able to assess writing is an important part of being able to write well. Without the ability to know when a piece of writing works or not, we would be unable to revise our writing or to respond to the feedback of others (Larson, 2000). This chapter makes a distinction between grading or testing students and using assessment to help students learn to work as writers. When we grade or test writing, the student receives some score, grade or label. Although the articulated judgment is based upon writing, the person is the object of that articulation. If, instead, we respond to the writing without a grade, score or label, then the writing remains the object. Testing and grading require an inference between the textual quality of the writing and the ability of the writer. In other words, a grade or test exists beyond our assessment of a particular text and beyond any commentary or instruction on how to improve the writing we are basing our judgments on in the first place. The purpose of grades or tests is to ascertain what a student knows or can do at a particular point. Grading or testing involves little or no learning or teaching. We need to conceive of writing assessment as a necessary, theoretical, authentic and practical part of the way we teach students to develop the complex tasks inherent in literate activity. As I detail later in chapter seven's discussion of assessment practices, when I talk about theory I am not talking about the creation of a grand scheme with great explanatory value—what I would call Theory with a capital T. Instead, I am concerned in this essay with the beliefs and assumptions that inform our practices— what I would call theory with a small t, what Gary Olson (1999) calls "theorizing."

My position, which is similar to James Zebroski's (1994), is that all of our practices are theoretically driven, since they are based upon our beliefs and assumptions. It's important, then, that we become more conscious of our theories concerning assessment and how they affect not only our assessment practices but the entire act of teaching writing. Louise Phelps's (1989) practice-theory-practice (PTP) arc describes the way in which practice and theory work dialectically to move forward both our practice and the theories that guide us as writing teacher practitioners. In Phelps's PTP arc, a practitioner starts with a specific practice (the first P) that she is unhappy with. Her goal is to arrive at a practice (the last P in the arc) with which she is more comfortable. However, before she can really change her practice, she must also confront the practice on a theoretical level. Donald Schön's notion of "reflection in action" frames practice as a knowledge-and-theory-building enterprise so that when the practitioner "reflects in action, he becomes a researcher in the practice context" (1983, 68). For Schön, framing the problem for reflection and reflective action is crucial. If we assume that testing, grading and assessment are automatically problematic, then there is no reason to examine these practices or our beliefs and assumptions about them. The problem is not in our thinking or practices. The problem is with assessment itself. On the other hand, if we assume "that in literate activity, assessment is everywhere," then we need to begin a reflective inquiry to examine the problem with the practices we now use in assessment and to suggest practices that are more consonant with our theories. Phelps's (1989) arc represents the ways in which reflection can propel practitioners toward new and better practices.

Assessing, testing or grading student writing is often framed as the worst aspect of the job of teaching student writers. Pat Belanoff describes grading as, "the dirty thing we have to do in the dark of our own offices" (1991, 61). Belanoff's lament about the dearth of material devoted to grading student writing appears to have been heard, since there are two recently published books about grades and college writing (Allison, Bryant and Hourigan 1999; Zak and Weaver 2000). These volumes are invaluable for those of us interested in grading, since the essays in these collections cover a wealth of issues including but not limited to power and grades (Bleich 1999; Elbow 2000), gender and grading (Papoulis 1999; Shiffman 1999), and historical perspectives on grades (Boyd 2000; Speck and Jones 2000). However rich these volumes are, none of the essays discuss the subject of grading in terms of its connection to wider issues of assessment and testing and their connections to teaching. Since grades and assessment signify what we value in instruction, connecting how and what we value to what we are attempting to teach seems crucial.

Traditionally, we have not attempted to distinguish among assessment, testing and grading, lumping them altogether under the heading of writing assessment. The classic definition of writing assessment from Leo Ruth and Sandra Murphy (1988), still in use, certainly makes no attempt to distinguish assessing from grading or testing student writing: "An assessment of writing occurs when a teacher, evaluator or researcher obtains information about a student's abilities in writing" (qtd. in. White, Lutz, and Kamuskiri 1996, 1). In fact, we might think that there is a deliberate attempt to connect the three, since the definition links teachers with evaluators or researchers, assuming that all three would want similar information about "a student's abilities in writing" or would go about getting this information in similar ways. There is also the assumption that assessment is always directed toward the abstract concept of "a student's ability in writing." At the heart of our profession's attitude toward assessment is a conception of it as a summative, generalized, rigid decision about a student writer based upon a first draft or single paper. Certainly this conception is bolstered by the use of a single, holistically scored writing sample that is often used to test writing outside of the classroom.

ASSESSING AND TEACHING

Our inability to distinguish among testing, grading and assessing or evaluating is one of the main reasons why teachers and students have misunderstood and devalued the pedagogical importance of writing evaluation. We have forgotten how important it is to be able to understand and appreciate the value of written expression and have instead focused on testing and grading student ability. For example, most summary comments on graded papers attempt to justify the grade (Connors and Lunsford 1993). Consequently, grading and testing are associated with assessment as an activity with no value for teaching or learning. The kind of assessment that exists outside of a context in which a student might improve her work can be labeled summative, whereas those judgments that allow the student to improve are called formative. Grades and tests, for the most part, are summative rather than formative because they consider a student text finished and its value fixed. This is a far cry from the type of judgments a teacher makes in reading student writing within an individual classroom—judgments that are based upon the context of the teaching moment in conjunction with the environment of the class and the history of her relationships with the student writer and her writing. In chapter five, I highlight the importance of the reading process, noting that instructor's ability to make meaning of a particular student's writing depends upon her experience in a specific classroom with a particular individual. Much of our evaluation or assessment as teachers, writers or editors is open, fluid, tentative and expectant—formative—as we work with a writer toward a potential text, recognizing the individual, textual purpose(s) of the writer. The type of judgment we know as grading has little relationship to the type of evaluation writers constantly make in the drafting of a particular piece of writing. Most writing instructors would agree that to grade individual drafts on a weekly basis misrepresents the process of writing as a cut and dried linear progression of publishable texts, without the reflection and recursion necessary for the creation of effective writing. I contend, however, that separating assessment from the process of composing equally misrepresents the writing process, since all of us who write have to make evaluative decisions and respond to others' assessments of our work (Larson, 2000).

To illustrate the contrasting sets of assumptions our practices hold, I look at some current traditional assessment practices and the assumptions behind such practices, contrasting them with some practices common in contemporary composition classrooms. Current traditional pedagogy emphasizes students' written products, which the instructor grades on a regular basis and averages into a course grade that reflects students' ability as writers. In a course in which students write papers for individual grades, even in instances where revision is encouraged, the instructor is completely responsible for assessment. When grades are equated with assessment—and this happens because of the power of grades in society and because grades are often the only evaluation students receive—then assessing the value of writing is completely erased from the student writing process. Why struggle with assigning value to your work when it will be thoroughly and often mysteriously judged by someone else? Even in the way we have constructed self assessment (see the second page of this chapter for examples and citations) student assessment has been focused on their grades or progress within a specific course. David Bleich (1999) illustrates the bureau-cratic role grades have always played. Unfortunately, this bureaucratic role has by default been assigned to assessment as well. As a result the context for revision, growth and self evalua-tion have always existed within the framework of being graded.

Returning graded and marked papers to students eliminates the need for response or defines it in very narrow, perfunctory terms, often encouraging students to rather perfunctory revi-sion. Instead of focusing on questions involving the improvement of a piece of writing, students are often focused on what will get them a desired grade, whether they think the revisions improve the writing or not. Writing papers for a grade creates a role for the student in which assessing the value of writing is secondary or moot and the attainment of a specific grade is everything. In this kind of assessment, students are accountable rather than respon-sible because grades come from a bureaucratic, higher authority over which they exert little or no control. Further, grades contex-tualize the evaluative moment. Instead of focusing on text, this kind of assessment focuses on students' ability to achieve a cer-tain grade which approximates an instructor's evaluation of their work rather than encouraging students to develop their own assessments about what they are writing. For students, then, writ-ing can become an elaborate game of getting the words right. Of course, the deleterious effects of writing for grades is not news. From Janet Emig's (1971) "school sponsored writing" to James Britton's (1975) "teacher as examiner," we have attempted to safeguard against the narrowing of literate activity to a meaning-less school exercise. However, we have yet to frame our under-standing in terms of assessment itself. Unless we teach students how to assess, we fail to provide them with the authority inherent in assessment, continuing the disjuncture between the compet-ing roles of student and writer. This conflict between the author-ity necessary to write well and the deference necessary to be a good student is nicely demonstrated in a research study in which professional writers receive lower holistic scores than students because professional writing violates the expectations teachers have for student work (Freedman 1984). Melanie Sperling and Sarah Freedman's (1987) study of the "Good Girl" demonstrates that in many writing classrooms the role of student consumes that of writer, with the student completing revisions she has no role in creating and effectively not learning how to make her own decisions about her writing.

Of course, newer models for teaching student writers attempt to decenter the writing classroom away from the teacher and toward the student, so she does, in fact, have the space and authority to work as a writer, reflecting the effort nec-essary to use the written word to make meaning. Typical class-room practices in contemporary classrooms include peer review, teacher-student conferences and portfolios. While each of these classroom activities gives students more responsibility and authority, they also require that students are able to assess texts—their own and others'—and are able to respond to the assessments of others for revision. However, many students are ill-equipped to make the kind of evaluative decisions about writ-ing which our pedagogy expects and often enter writing courses with strict, text-based notions of how to judge writing. A crucial missing element in most writing pedagogy is any experience or instruction in ascertaining the value of one's own work. It is common for teachers to have to make sure that initial peer review sessions not focus entirely upon mechanical correctness. It is also common for students to hand in their first paper for response with a brave "rip it up" or to insist that teachers tell them which papers should be revised or included in a portfolio. These common classroom scripts illustrate a gap between the kinds of evaluative abilities our pedagogy expects and those our students bring with them. These scripts also illustrate the serious gaps between our theories and practices for assessment and some of the more common practices for the teaching of writing. Current classroom practices require evaluative skills from students which we do not, for the most part, teach.

The lack of a conscious and critical understanding about the value of assessment appears to drive an overall misunderstanding about the role of assessment in teaching writing. Our students carry with them many of the negative, critical, correctness-centered notions of evaluation that are so prevalent in society and among their writing instructors. Students' emphasis on the connection of evaluation to surface-level correctness in writing might be related to their focus on mechanical concerns in revision. Assessment, grading and testing have often overemphasized the importance of correctness, while at the same time they have ignored the importance of rhetorical features of writing. Certainly, most writing teachers see the need for instruction and emphasis on grammatical and rhetorical aspects of writing. However, what we assess, grade or test ultimately determines what we value. It is not surprising, then, that most student revision centers on correctness, since the value of correct writing has been emphasized over and over again in various assessment, testing and grading contexts. We need to recognize that before students can learn to revise rhetorically, they need to assess rhetorically. Certainly much current writing instruction focuses on rhetorical concepts, but there is no clear evidence that our assessment of student writing focuses on these same criteria. In fact, large scale research into teacher response (Connors and Lunsford 1993) as well as classroom-based research (Sperling 1994) seems to indicate that teachers do not respond to and evaluate student writing rhetorically. Assessing student writing rhetorically and teaching students to assess rhetorically does not seem to be an insurmountable task, but it will require a more conscious effort to focus our evaluations on how students attend to rhetorical concepts in their writing. Just as we have had to rethink the teaching of writing as a process, we also need to rethink what it means for our students to evaluate the way writing works and to relate these decisions about writing quality to the process of writing itself.

This rethinking requires that we begin developing a pedagogy for assessment with our students that focuses on their writing and the choices writers make. Assessment as a way to teach and learn writing requires more than just feedback on writing in progress from a teacher or peer group. It is common to distinguish between summative evaluation given at the end of the writing process and formative evaluation, given while a writer is still working. What I'm calling for can probably best be labeled *instructive evaluation,* since it is tied to the act of learning a specific task while participating in a particular literacy event. Instructive evaluation involves the student in the process of evaluation, making her aware of what it is she is trying to create and how well her current draft matches the linguistic and rhetorical targets she has set for herself, targets that have come from her understanding of the context, audience, purpose and other rhetorical features of a specific piece of writing. Instructive evaluation requires that we involve the student in all phases of the assessment of her work. We must help her set the rhetorical and linguistic targets that will best suit her purpose in writing and then we have to help her evaluate how well she has met such targets, using this evaluation to help her reach additional targets and set new ones. While the conscious setting of such targets requires the ability to understand the rhetorical nature of literate communication, the attainment of these rhetorical aims requires the ability to assess specific language forms and be able to create those forms to which the writer and her audience assign value.

Instructive evaluation demands that students and teachers connect the ability to assess with the necessity to revise, creating a motivation for revision that is often so difficult for students to obtain. So many aspects of writing, from the initial planning stages of audience assessment to decisions about the right word during editing and proofreading, depend upon our ability to evaluate. Being able to assess writing quality and to know what works in a particular rhetorical situation are important tools for all writers. Instructive evaluation can also work to mitigate the gap between the often competing roles of student and writer, since instruction in evaluating writing gives students the rights and responsibilities that only teachers have in traditional writing classrooms. A classroom pedagogy that encourages and high-lights the evaluative decisions of writers, teachers, and peer review groups can help foster a new, shared role for assessment and the teaching of writing. Sandra Murphy (1997, 86) argues for the use of assessment in teaching, providing examples from three K-12 classrooms. In one classroom, students evaluate samples of writing, ranking them and providing criteria for each ranking. The discussion is synthesized on a handout given to students. In another classroom, students create wall charts of features of good writing, revising them throughout the year as their ideas about writing evolve. And finally, students and teachers generate lists of statements about what makes good writing, and this list is used by students selecting pieces for their portfolios. In each of these sce-narios, students learn to write by learning how to assess. Thus, instructive evaluation combines assessment with learning how to write. Just as the process movement helped writing instructors learn to teach writing as more than just a finished product, so too the concept of instructive evaluation allows students to see assess-ment as more than just what teachers do to their texts. Students learn to use assessment to improve their own writing and to progress as writers. The ability and responsibility for assessment is something that good writers understand, and it is something all successful writers need to learn. Instructive evaluation casts the act of assessment as an important component for learning critical aspects about the process of writing. Instructive evaluation also requires different kinds of classroom roles for students and teachers in which all assessments are linked to helping writers improve.

PORTFOLIOS

Of all writing assessments used in and out of the classroom, none have generated more interest and enthusiasm among writing teachers than the portfolio. Portfolios have the potential to disrupt the prevailing negative attitudes toward assessment and its adverse effects on teaching and learning. They are one of the few assessment practices that have their roots within the classroom, potentially providing students with a more representative and realistic concept of writing evaluation and helping them acquire the types of assessment skills important and necessary for evaluating and responding to suggestions for revision. If we use portfolios in a conscious attempt to combine teaching and assessment, they can work to provide new potential for assessment in and about the writing classroom. However, unless we exploit and recognize the shift in assessment theory that drives portfolios, they will end up being just another tool for organizing student writing within the classroom, a sort of glorified checklist through which students are judged according to the number of texts produced at certain times throughout the semester. In another words, if we continue to see portfolios as just another way of testing, grading or even teaching writing, then their potential to fundamentally transform assessment in the writing classroom will be lost. A primary consideration for portfolios is that they help us to see assessment in a new light, one that connects teaching and assessment. Just as we must learn to utilize assessment in our teaching, we should not ignore the assessment properties of portfolios. Because portfolios can alter the relationship between grading and evaluation in the composition classroom, it is imperative that we become conscious of the theoretical consequences involved in grading student writing before it has the opportunity to become part of a portfolio.

Portfolios are part of a tradition in the visual and performing arts that looks at multiple products and processes, hoping to discover and document the progress of an individual student or learner. The theory driving the shift to portfolios in writing assessment demands that we think differently about evaluation. Portfolios undermine the current assumption that it is possible to ascertain a student's ability to write from one piece of writing, or that writing or a writer's development can be inferred incrementally through the evaluation of individual products or an aggregate of individual evaluations. It is fair to say that collecting, selecting and reflecting, three of the major activities involved in portfolio compilation (Yancey 1992), are also acts of assessment, since students make their decisions based upon an assessment of their own writing.

Certainly, the assumptions behind grading and testing are that student ability can and should be measured by the sum of the scores received on individual tasks or assignments. Portfolios provide the student and teacher with a variety of writing samples that can only be understood and evaluated in context and relationship with each other. A judgment based on a student's portfolio can radically differ from a judgment based on an individual student text, because it includes a range of contextual factors—including but not limited to the other texts in the portfolio, the act of selecting pieces for inclusion, any writing about texts and the process of writing, and compiling the portfolio. The variety of texts within a portfolio accounts for the progressive, developmental and fluid nature of written language acquisition. The texts in a portfolio typically devoted to reflection and writing about writing focus not only on the product of writing but on the process as well, demonstrating what the student writer knows about the product and process of writing within her own experience as a writer. Thus, the act of writing and the ability to talk about that writing promote a pedagogy that emphasizes not only the writing the student produces and the process that generates that writing, but also the student's development as a writer.

For the most part, the scholarly literature on portfolios has focused so far on what constitutes a portfolio and how it can be used. However, Sandra Murphy (1994) and others have reminded us that the way portfolios are used is a key feature for harnessing their potential. For example, it is possible to use portfolios within the same theoretical framework that underlies testing and grading by assigning separate numbers or letters to individual papers within a portfolio. This is a common practice because while it is relatively easy to switch to portfolios, it is much more difficult to alter the assumptions behind our practices. If however, we want to conceive of portfolios as a viable way to improve how we assess student writing, then we need to consider them as discrete units about which we can assign value.

Grading, even in a portfolio, freezes student work and teacher commentary. Ungraded but responded-to writing in a portfolio directs the articulation of judgment toward the evolving written product rather than at the student writer, giving students an opportunity to explore, experiment and compose across a body of work without receiving a summative evaluation of their effort. When teachers articulate their judgments with grades, students can feel that they are the objects of this assessment, since they ultimately receive the grade. In a portfolio context, grade-free commentary is targeted at the writing the student is still potentially able to revise before he or she becomes the target of the assessment through grades. This redirection of teacher judgment can alter student focus away from their grades and their current identity as students and toward their writing and the writers they can become. Portfolios reduce the number of moments within a course when teachers test or grade their students' work. This reduction in the number of times teachers have to grade can not only free them to do more teaching, but it can also alter their roles within the classroom, making them more responsive and editorial and less judgmental and adversarial. Introducing grades into portfolio practice can fracture their underlying theoretical assumptions. Grades on individual papers can undermine an essential tenet of portfolio theory:

that works produced by a person cannot be judged individually, incrementally or outside the context of other texts with which they were written.

To harness the transformative power that portfolios can furnish, a student should be graded only at the end of an appropriate instructional period designed by an instructor, and this grade should take into consideration her ability with a range of rhetorical and linguistic tasks. As an assessment device, portfolios can exist outside current traditional assessment theory and practice only if they disrupt the practice of automatically assigning grades to each paper. Recognizing the portfolio as a unit of assessment requires that no judgments be made until the portfolio is complete or at a juncture when an instructor has made a conscious decision to give a grade to a specific amount of student writing. What seems to be important in using portfolios is that an instructor consciously decides when a student should receive graded feedback and that this decision should be a part of the instructional goals of the course, whether the grade(s) come at the end, middle or some other time during a school semester or quarter. In this way, portfolios provide a means for distinguishing between testing or grading and assessment, furnishing the potential for truly transforming assessment as it works to dispel prevailing beliefs and assumptions that link testing, grading and assessing writing. Instead of all teacher judgment being coded as grades and the plethora of personal and cultural baggage they contain, students receive teacher judgment as response directed toward specific rhetorical and linguistic features of their writing.

In addition to approaching the evaluative properties of portfolios through the same lens that guides more traditional notions of grading and testing, portfolios have also been seen primarily in terms of their ability to promote the teaching of writing, keeping intact the notion that assessment is detrimental to the teaching and learning of writing. The move to separate portfolios from the assessment of student writing is symptomatic of the larger, problematic relationship between the teaching and assessing of writing. This separation allows composition practitioners to continue to ignore an examination of the "dirty thing we do in the dark of our offices" (Belanoff 1991, 61). Making us more conscious of our theories about assessing writing and establishing assessment as a necessary component for effective writing curricula are some of the most important contributions portfolios can make to the teaching of writing. To conceive of portfolios separately as instruments for teaching and as means for assessing not only ignores our most "pressing challenge," but it also promotes the continuing rift between the way we assess and the way we teach. If portfolios are going to be more than another educational fad (Elbow 1994; Huot 1994), we need to do our best to link the theories behind them with our practices in the classroom. Portfolios furnish the pedagogical context in which teachers can evaluate student writing as part of the way they teach. Most importantly, portfolios allow the possibility of not only changing teachers' grading and assessment practices but of altering the theoretical foundation which informs such practice, providing a pedagogy for assessment free of grading and testing.

USING ASSESSMENT TO TEACH WRITING

Although composition teachers are often urged to be less evaluative of their students, Peter Elbow (1993) points out that it is not evaluation per se that is the problem, but rather the type and frequency of evaluative decisions we make about students' writing. He draws our attention to the multidimensional nature of evaluation, arguing that we as teachers need to pay more attention to describing and liking student writing than to ranking it against the efforts of others. Elbow's ideas for changing teacher practice recognize the different kinds of assessment decisions a teacher can make and the complexity involved in arriving at decisions concerning the value of student text. Elbow points out for us that there are many ways to look at assessment. For some, like those who advocate "authentic" assessment, the often-condemned practice of teaching to the test is only wrong because of the nature of our tests (Wiggins, 1993).

Elbow's practical advice and other congruent practices are supported by a range of theories about assessment and assigning value to texts. Like Elbow, Grant Wiggins feels the answer is not to eliminate assessment from the curriculum but to change the way we assess. Wiggins's ideas are part of a movement in educational assessment that recognizes the importance of evaluation in education and the lack of relevance and value in much of the way we now evaluate student ability. According to Pamela Moss, this movement, which includes "performative" assessment, is composed of "extended discourse, work exhibits, portfolios or other products or performances" (1992, 229). Moss goes on to say "This expanding interest in performative assessment reflects the growing consensus among educators about the impact of evaluation on what students learn and what teachers teach." (1992, 229). It should be noted that although performance and authentic assessment are often used interchangeably, they do point to two distinct sets of practices (see Black, Helton, and Sommers 1994 for definitions and discussions of these two movements).

Other alternative assessment theorists like Peter Johnston (1989) question the notion of objectivity, contending that the personal involvement necessary for successful learning can never be appreciated through so-called objective means of assessment. Patricia Carini (1994; 2001), who has been pioneering alternative assessment for over a quarter of a century, questions the whole apparatus of assessment, emphasizing the importance of describing rather than evaluating student progress. Carini draws upon theories of phenomenology and hermeneutics, suggesting that it is only through communal and shared reflective discourse that we can truly appreciate student progress and therefore learn to find where students are available for instruction. Lester Faigley (1989) provides us with a dramatic illustration of subjectivity and assigning value in a postmodern world by comparing the type of decisions made by evaluators of the College Entrance Examination Board in the 1930s with judgments made by compositionists in the mid 1980s. Although judgment issues can vary widely, according to Faigley what remains the same is the construction of a particular, valued self for students who receive favor or condemnation. These various positions concerning assessment complicate the role of any central authority or standard to know the "real" value of a student text or writer. These positions also foreground the important but neglected fact that before we can evaluate any text we must first read it, a point I examine more fully in chapter five. They also open up the possibility of seeing assessment as something that can be shared, as hermeneutic (Allen 1995; Barritt, Stock, and Clark 1986; Broad 2000; Carini 2001; Moss 1996; and others), when a group of interested people search for values and meaning through group interpretation (see Barritt, Stock, and Clark 1986; Carini 2001; Durst, Roemer, and Schultz 1994; Himley 1989 for examples of communal assessment practices).

To harness peer review, portfolios, or any classroom activity to teach and promote students' ability to critically evaluate writing, we must make assessment an explicit part of the writing classroom. While portfolios can be used to encourage students to write and reflect about the decisions they are making about their writing, an emphasis on assessment attempts to make this process more conscious and visible. Ask most student writers why they did or did not make certain initial decisions or revisions, and you're not likely to receive a very well developed or thoughtful response. Without an understanding of the ways in which good writers assess the progress of their writing, our students are ill equipped to make the kinds of evaluative decisions necessary for good writing. While more current approaches to the teaching of writing give students freedom in choosing topics, getting feedback, and working through a process they can control, they also generate more responsibility for the student who must be able to assess her progress at various junctures.

There are, however, many ways in which assessment can become a more integral part of our pedagogy. For example, reflective material for a portfolio could focus explicitly on the assessment criteria and the entire process of evaluating specific pieces of texts. Students would use those judgments to make further decisions about revision, articulating and becoming conscious of the values they hold for effective communication. This individual reflection could lead specifically to classroom discussions and activities that revolve around what features make effective writing. Many teachers develop with their students scoring guidelines not unlike those used in holistic scoring sessions, so that students know what to look for and expect from teacher-assessment of their work. Individual students can be helped to develop specific assessment criteria for each piece they write, encouraging them to set and assess criteria for each essay. Student-teacher conferences can focus on passages of student writing that they identify as strong or weak. Using assessment to teach requires the additional steps of having students apply discussions of writing quality to their individual texts or compile criteria for individual papers that they can discuss with a teacher or peer group. Students can only learn the power of assessment as they can other important features of learning to write—within the context of their own work. Learning how to assess entails more than applying stock phrases like *unity*, *details*, *development*, or *organization* to a chart or scoring guideline. Students and teachers can use these ideas to talk about the rhetorical demands of an emergent text, so that students could learn how to develop their own critical judgments about writing. This creation of a classroom pedagogy for assessment should provide students with a clearer idea about how text is evaluated, and it should work against the often nebulous, undeveloped, and unarticulated ideas they have about why they like a certain piece of writing or make certain revisions.

CONCLUSION

Using assessment to teach writing means more than highlighting evaluative decisions about texts. It means teaching students the process of assessment, and this means teaching them how to read and describe what they have read. Carini's (1994; 2001) method for reflective conversation involves an initial descriptive stage in which readers must paraphrase and describe what a text attempts to convey. This ability to describe is something students often find quite difficult, as they often attempt to move prematurely and uncritically to an evaluative decision about a text. When I have limited students to descriptive comments in responding to either a published piece of writing or an essay written by a student in class, usually I have had to explain more than once that no comment with any evaluation is acceptable. Students often have trouble eliminating evaluative language from the commentary, since phrases like "I like," "good," "didn't like," and so forth are often an unconscious part of the ways our students think and talk about writing. Once students learn to voice other kinds of comments, they often find themselves reading more deeply and precisely, finding things in a piece of writing they might otherwise miss. Having students describe a text before giving a writer feedback often improves the quality and the kinds of comments they can make. Richard Larson (2000) notes the difficulty a writer has in seeing her own text as a genuine site for rethinking and revision. Having students learn to describe their own texts during the process of revision helps them achieve the often elusive objectivity writers struggle with in rewriting. Learning to describe what one sees in a text is an important part of being able to develop the critical consciousness necessary for a developed, evaluative sense about writing. Seeing the ability to assess as a process links it to the writing process and embeds assessment within the process of learning to write.

Articulating a new understanding for grading, testing, teaching and assessing student writing is an ambitious goal. Any substantive change in the way we think, practice and talk about assessment demands a change in our beliefs, assumptions and attitudes concerning assessment and its role in the classroom. Facing the reality that assessment is an important part of writing and its teaching leaves us little choice but to learn to use assessment in new ways, helping students to assess their writing as they learn to write in various, and demanding contexts. This re-articulation of assessment and its attendant practices will distinguish between grading, testing and assessing writing and will help to find ways to use the portfolio for assessment and teaching. I hope this chapter also draws us into new conversations about assessment and the teaching of writing, conversations that eventually help us to put assessment in its proper place, focusing both the student's and teacher's attention on the development of texts and of the student as a writer.

4
TOWARD A NEW THEORY OF WRITING ASSESSMENT

Many writing teachers and scholars feel frustrated by, cut off from, or otherwise uninterested in the subject of writing assessment, especially assessment that takes place outside of the classroom for purposes of placement, exit, or program evaluation. This distrust and estrangement are understandable, given the highly technical aspects of much discourse about writing assessment. For the most part, writing assessment has been developed, constructed, and privatized by the measurement community as a technological apparatus whose inner workings are known only to those with specialized knowledge. Consequently, English professionals have been made to feel inadequate and naive by considerations of technical concepts like validity and reliability. At the same time, teachers have remained skeptical, and rightly so, of assessment practices that do not reflect the values important to an understanding of how people learn to read and write. It does not take a measurement specialist to realize that many writing assessment procedures have missed the mark in examining students' writing ability.

Many current debates about writing assessment issues (like whether or not to use standardized or local procedures for assessment, or whether or not we should abandon single-sample assessment in favor of portfolios) occur within a theoretical vacuum. Basically, we talk about and compare practices which have no articulated underlying theoretical foundation. Consequently, there are those scholars in composition who have questioned whether writing assessment is a theoretical enterprise at all. Anne Ruggles Gere (1980) suggested that writing assessment lacks a theoretical foundation; Faigley, Cherry, Jolliffe and Skinner (1985) elaborate this view by explaining that the pressing need to develop writing assessment procedures outstrips our ability to develop a theoretical basis for them.

My purpose in this chapter is to consider writing assessment from a theoretical perspective. By looking at the underlying principles which inform current practices, it is possible to consider how our beliefs and assumptions about teaching can and should inform the way we approach writing evaluation. I argue that, contrary to some scholarly opinion, writing assessment has always been a theory-driven practice. After tracing this theoretical thread to roots in classical test theory and its positivist assumptions, I illustrate how this theory has worked during the past couple of decades by examining current practices. These current practices and their underlying theoretical position are made all the more problematic if we consider the radical shift in testing theory that has been going on for the last two decades or so. This revolution in assessment theory has fostered performative approaches to assessment like the portfolio but, more importantly, it has actually redefined what it means for a test to be a valid measure of student ability. I express the need for the articulation of a new set of theoretical assumptions and practices for writing assessment. This theory will need to reconcile theoretical issues in measurement like validity and reliability with theoretical concerns in composition like rhetorical context and variable textual interpretations.

THEORETICAL FOUNDATION OF WRITING ASSESSMENT

Essentially, it is a mistake to assume that writing assessment has been developed outside the confines of a theoretical construct. While the field of composition often dates its birth in the 1960s, with the publication of *Research in Written Composition* or the convening of the Dartmouth Conference, work in writing assessment goes back several decades before that. Entrance examinations, implemented by Harvard and other universities before the turn of the twentieth century, were influenced during the 1920s by advances in educational testing brought on by the need to classify recruits for WWI, and were used to formalize writing assessment under the auspices of such testing institutions as the College Entrance Examination Board (CEEB). The development of writing assessment procedures, as we now know them, are the result of decades of research by the test development staff at CEEB and the Educational Testing Service (ETS). Building upon research started in the twenties (Hopkins 1921), the researchers at CEEB and ETS systematically established the procedures for writing assessment. (See Godshalk, Swineford and Coffman 1966 for a review of this literature.)

These efforts were undertaken under the auspices of classical test theory, which dictates that a measurement instrument has to be both valid and reliable. Classical test theory is based on a positivist philosophy which contends "that there exists a reality *out there*, driven by immutable natural laws" (Guba 1990, 19). Within the positivist foundation of classical test theory, it is possible to isolate a particular human ability, like writing, and measure it. Positivist reality assumes that student ability in writing, as in anything else, is a fixed, consistent, and acontextual human trait. Our ability to measure such a trait would need to recognize these consistencies and could be built upon psychometrics, a statistical apparatus devised for use in the social and hard sciences. Mathematics, as in physics, was conceived as the "language" of an empirical methodology that would assist in the discovery of fundamental laws governing human behavior. Guba (1990) labels this science "context free," because the laws revealed by this type of scientific method are held to be independent of the observer and the particular events in which they were discovered. Within such a paradigm, for example, the scores that students receive on a writing test like the National Assessment of Educational Progress (NAEP) are an accurate measure of the writing ability of the nation's students.[1] The results represent students' ability to write and can be compared from school to school and year to year, since psychometric methods ensure that their meaning exists outside of the context or time in which they were generated.

One of the reasons for writing scholars' belief that writing assessment is atheoretical stems from the fact that it was developed outside of the theoretical traditions that are normally considered part of composition. In addition to psychometricians at ETS, researchers trained to prepare secondary English teachers were responsible for much of the early work in writing assessment. Traditionally, an important aspect of the typical graduate program for English teachers is at least one or more courses in psychometric theory and practice. However, in the 1980s, as the study of writing became an interest for researchers trained in the humanities-based disciplines of rhetoric and composition (as opposed to the social sciences tradition of educational research), experimental and quantitative approaches to research became less important. Most researchers studying writing, without training in psychometric theory, were not aware of the theoretical origins of writing assessment. Most of them saw such concerns as the consistency (reliability) of assessment techniques simply as a matter of fairness (White 1993). Thus, issues that had originally been theoretical became pragmatic, and writing assessment became an apparently atheoretical endeavor.

The use of student writing to measure writing ability was unsupportable within classical test theory until the 1960s, because testing developers were unable until that time to devise methods for furnishing agreement among independent raters on the same paper. The theoretical foundation of writing assessment is apparent in our continuing emphasis on ensuring reliable methods for scoring student writing. Simply, interrater reliability has dominated writing assessment literature, a point I made in chapter two when referring to the overwhelming amount of research on reliability. As I noted, however, this trend has been changing a little during the past few years, as scholarship on writing assessment has begun to move beyond just establishing the procedures themselves. It is clear from even a cursory reflection on the history of direct writing assessment that not only were current methods for evaluation created within an established disciplinary framework, but that critical issues like reliability and validity existed and were defined within the context of classical test theory. The inability of scholars in composition to recognize the theoretical connections in writing assessment practices comes from the fact that it is a theory which has little familiarity or relevance for most people who teach and study the teaching of writing, especially at the college level. It is also possible to understand that our dissatisfaction with conventional means for assessing student writing (Broad 1994, 2000; Charney 1984; Faigley, Cherry, Jolliffe, and Skinner 1985; Gere 1980) has more to do with the theory that it informs it than with the practice of assessing student writing itself.

CURRENT PRACTICE IN WRITING ASSESSMENT

To be a viable option within classical test theory, writing assessment had to meet the same requirements expected of standardized tests. Conventional writing assessment's emphasis on uniformity and test-type conditions are a product of a testing theory that assumes that individual matters of context and rhetoric are factors to be overcome. From this perspective, a "true" measure of student ability can only be achieved through technical and statistical rigor. Most of the procedures and improvements in writing assessment have had as their goals either the reliability of the scoring or of the instrument itself. For example, writing assessment requires the development of writing prompts that are similar in difficulty and suitability for the testing population. Some early writing assessment programs produced great discrepancies in scores from one year to another because the writing tasks were of such variable difficulty (Hoetker 1982). Procedures for designing appropriate writing prompts often involve pilot testing and other measures (Ruth and Murphy 1988)[2] that ensure that students will perform fairly consistently on writing tasks used as part of the same or similar programs across different locations and times.

The bulk of writing assessment procedures are devoted to furnishing the raters with a means for agreement (Davis, Scriven, and Thomas 1987; Myers 1980; White 1994). Generally, raters are trained on a set of sample papers that are especially representative of particular scores on a scoring guideline or rubric. Once raters can agree consistently on scores for sample papers, they begin to score independently on "real, live papers." Raters are periodically retrained or calibrated each day and throughout the scoring session(s) at appropriate intervals like after breaks for meals. These practices are consistent with a theory that assumes that teachers or other experts can identify good writing when they see it, and that in order for the assessment to be valid it must be consistent.

Within the positivist assumptions that construct and rely on the technology of testing, there is no need for different sets of procedures depending upon context, because writing ability is a fixed and isolated human trait, and this ability or quality can be determined though an analysis of various textual features. Depending on our purposes or resources, we can assess holistically for a general impression of quality, analytically for specific traits endemic to writing quality, or with a primary trait approach which treats rhetorical features of the writing assignment as the traits to be evaluated. Through the use of various scoring guidelines, we can decide what is of value within a student text and can base our judgments of a student's writing upon differing approaches to that text. The assumption underlying these procedures is that writing quality exists within the text. See Figure 1 for a summary of the assumptions underlying traditional writing assessment procedures. While analytic (Freedman 1984) and primary trait (Veal and Hudson 1983) are usually considered a little better than holistic measures, holistic is cheapest and therefore considered the most popular (Veal and Hudson 1983).

Regardless of which form of writing assessment we choose to use, the emphasis is on the formal aspects of the procedures, the training of raters, the construction of scoring guidelines, the techniques necessary to guarantee interrater reliability. This emphasis is consonant with the importance of reliability in testing theory: "reliability is a necessary but not a sufficient condition for validity" (Cherry and Meyer 1993, 110). This importance for reliability has been adopted by college writing assessment

Figure 1

*Traditional Writing Assessment
Procedures, Purposes and Assumptions*

PROCEDURE	PURPOSE	ASSUMPTION
scoring guideline	recognize features of writing quality	writing quality can be defined and determined
rater training	foster agreement on independent rater scores	one set of features of student writing for which raters should agree
scores on papers	fix degree of writing quality for comparing writing ability and making decisions on that ability	student ability to write can be coded and communicated numerically
interrater reliability	calculate the degree of agreement between independent raters	consistency and standardization to be maintained across time and location
validity	determine that the assessment measures what it purports to measure	an assessment's value is limited to distinct goals and properties in the instrument itself

specialists and equated with fairness. Edward White provides a good summary of this position: "Reliability is a simple way of talking about fairness to test takers, and if we are not interested in fairness, we have no business giving tests or using test results" (1993, 93). Logically, then, the same procedures which ensure consistency should also provide fairness. However, this is not the case. First of all, we need to understand that reliability indicates only how consistent an assessment is. "Reliability refers to how consistently a test measures whatever it measures . . . a test can be reliable but not be valid" (Cherry and Meyer 1993, 110). For example, I could decide to measure student writing by counting the number of words in each essay (in fact a computer could count the words). This method could achieve perfect interrater reliability, since it is possible that two independent judges would count the same number of words for each paper. While reliable, we could hardly consider the method to be a fair evaluation of student writing. In order for an assessment instrument to be fair, we must know something about the nature of the judgment itself. Translating "reliability" into "fairness" is not only inaccurate, it is dangerous, because it equates the statistical consistency of the judgments being made with their value. While I applaud and agree with White's contention that writing assessment needs to be fair, and I agree that consistency is a component of fairness, there is nothing within current assessment procedures which addresses, let alone ensures, fairness.

Within the theory which currently drives writing assessment, the criteria for judging student writing are not an explicit part of assessment procedures. George Engelhard Jr., Belita Gordon and Stephen Gabrielson (1992) give us an example of a theoretically acceptable study of writing evaluation which contains some questionable criteria for assessing student writing. The study reports on the writing of 127,756 eighth-grade students and draws conclusions about the effects of discourse mode, experiential demand, and gender on writing quality. Three out of the five domains used for scoring all of this writing are "sentence formation," "usage" and "mechanics." The other two domains also emphasize the conventions of writing. "Content and organization" are relegated to one domain, with "clearly established controlling idea," "clearly discernible order of presentation" and "logical transitions and flow of ideas" as three of the six items in the domain. It is pretty easy to see how applicable these items are to the form of the standard five-paragraph essay. Domain number two, which is labeled "style," also focuses on the forms of writing. Although two of the items list "concrete images and descriptive language, [and] appropriate tone for topic, audience, and purpose," the other two are "easily readable [and] varied sentence patterns." While the study reports the results domain by domain, there is no attempt to differentiate the value of scores for content and organization over those for mechanics (1992, 320). What this research really reports is how the conventions and mechanics of student writing relate to the categories of analyses. This study might more easily and cheaply find out similar things about students by administering tests of grammar and mechanics with a question or two thrown in on thesis statements, topic sentences and transitions. However, the use of an essay test carries with it the weight or illusion of a higher degree of validity. Since the scoring of student writing follows recognizable procedures and produces acceptable levels of interrater reliability, there are no reasons under current traditional theories for assessment to question the study's results. Consequently, it was published in one of the profession's most prestigious journals.

My last example of current practices in writing assessment comes from a roundtable on reliability in writing assessment at a national convention during the 1990s. All of the presenters at the session were employed by testing companies. Two of the presenters (Joan Chikos Auchter 1993; Michael Bunch and Henry Scherich 1993) report using a set number of sample papers which had been given the same score by a large board of raters as their "true score or validity." Raters are trained to give the same score, and their suitability as raters depends upon their ability to match the score of the board. "The common characteristic of all of our readers is that they understand and accept the fact that they will score essays according to someone else's standards" (Bunch and Scherich 1993, 2). While such methods are effective in producing high interrater reliability, they are questionable even within psychometric theory. Validity is supposed to be separate from reliability, and here it is conflated for the set purpose of ensuring consistency in scoring. "True score" (for a good discussion relevant to writing assessment, see White 1994) is the score an examinee would get on a test if she could take it an infinite number of times; it would perfectly reflect her ability. The notion of true score used by these companies has nothing to do with a student's ability. Instead, the focus is directed to the scores she receives. True score becomes the number of scores the student gets on the same test, her ability forever fixed and accurate on one writing assignment because it is scored by many individuals. This last example of current practices in writing assessment is probably an extreme case, abusing the very theory that drives it. However, these practices are considered reputable and are used to make important educational decisions about students. One of these companies alone reports scoring three million student essays per year (Bunch and Scherich 1993, 3)—a number that has and will probably continue to increase, given the proliferation of state-mandated writing assessments in the 1990s and the impending federal assessments of public schools.

These practices and the theory that drive them are all the more lamentable when we consider that assessment theory has been undergoing a theoretical revolution during the last two decades, a revolution which has yet to filter down to the assessment of student writing. For example, in a report on the validity of the Vermont portfolio system, delivered at a national convention on measurement, the presenter elected to ignore more recent definitions of validity which also consider a test's influence on teaching and learning because "it would muddy the water" (Koretz 1993). Instead, he concentrated his remarks on the low interrater reliability coefficients and the consequently suspect validity of portfolio assessment in Vermont. What makes this type of scholarship in writing assessment even more frustrating is that portfolios are a form of performative assessment and are exactly the kind of practice that newer conceptions of validity are designed to support (Moss 1992). However, if we apply the more traditional, positivist notions of validity and reliability, we are judging a practice (portfolios, in this case) from outside the theoretical basis that informs it.

RECENT DEVELOPMENTS IN TESTING THEORY

It is necessary for those of us who teach writing and work in writing assessment to examine some of the radical shifts in testing theory which have been emerging, because these shifts have been influenced by the same philosophical and theoretical movements in the construction of knowledge that have influenced writing pedagogy. Some extreme positions call for the dismantling of validity itself, the cornerstone of classical test theory. For example, Guba and Lincoln (1989), in their book *Fourth Generation Evaluation*, posit a theory of evaluation based on the tenets of social construction in which validity is seen as just another social construct. Peter Johnston contends "that the term validity as it is used in psychometrics needs to be taken off life support" (1989, 510). Harold Berlak (1992) elaborates validity's insupportable position of privilege in testing.

> validity as a technical concept is superfluous. . . . I should point out that abandoning validity as a technical concept does not automatically mean abandoning all standardized and criterion referenced tests. It does mean, however, that [they] . . . may no longer be privileged as "scientific;" their usefulness and credibility are to be judged alongside any other form of assessment practice. (186)

These critiques of validity are critiques of a positivist notion of reality that assumes that human traits are distributed normally throughout the population and that these traits are distinct from the observer or tester and can thus be measured accurately across individual contexts. In fact, the power of psychometric procedures lies in their ability to render results that are accurate and generalizable to the population at large. These underlying positivist postures toward reality which inform traditional testing are partly responsible for the importance that objectivity and outside criteria for judging writing have in our thinking about the testing of writing. Judgments about student writing are often questioned as not being objective enough.

According to Johnston, the notion of objectivity in testing is linked to the positivist philosophy that has tightened the psychometric grip on educational testing.

> The search for objectivity in psychometrics has been a search for tools that will provide facts that are untouched by human minds. Classical measurement has enshrined objectivity in terms such as "objective" tests and "true score" (absolute reality) . . . The point is that no matter how we go about educational evaluation, it involves interpretation. Human symbol systems are involved, and thus there is no "objective" measurement. (1989, 510)

Johnston notes that even in the hard sciences the act of observation can alter what is being observed. For example, when light is used to view atomic particles, what we see is altered because of the effect of the light on what is observed. In his chapter on the history of writing assessment, Michael Williamson gives us another example which illustrates that reality is often an illusive quality even in science. He points out that an instrument like a telescope only gives the illusion of direct observation. "In fact, a telescope magnifies the light or radio waves reflected or emitted by cosmic bodies and does not result in direct observation at all" (Williamson 1993, 7).

In his discussion of objectivity, Johnston goes on to explain that in assessing students' abilities to read and write, interpretation plays an even larger role because communication depends on personal commitment, and texts cannot exist outside of the context and history in which they are produced. While those of us who teach writing have always known that we could only pretend to assess writing from an "objective" stance and therefore deferred to testing specialists for an objective view, Johnston contends that, "The search for objectivity may not simply be futile. I believe it to be destructive" (1989, 511). Drawing upon the work of Jerome Bruner, Johnston explains that if education is to create a change in individuals beyond the ability to regurgitate information, its focus cannot be "objective," because abilities like creativity, reflection, and critical thinking require a personal relationship with the subject. This negative influence of objectivity relates specifically to the assessment of writing, since good communication often requires the personal involvement of both writer and reader. The importance of reflection or point of view in writing is contradictory to an objective approach, because to assume a particular position is to be subjective (Johnston 1989, 511). New movements in testing theory which question the advisability of devising objective tests and maintaining equally objective evaluations of student performance have important implications for writing assessment, since those of us who teach and research literacy have always known that writing assessment could never be totally objective, and that writing which approached such objectivity would not be effective communication.

Although the diminishing need for objectivity will have an important effect on writing assessment, the biggest change will eventually be felt in developing notions of validity. For several decades, stretching back to the 1950s, validity has come to be defined as more than just whether or not a test measures what it purports to measure. Samuel Messick (1989a; 1989b) and Lee Cronbach (1988; 1989), two of the most prominent scholars of validity theory, revised their views throughout the 1980s. For Messick, validity is "an integrated evaluative judgment of the degree to which empirical evidence and theoretical rationales support the adequacy and appropriateness of inferences and actions based on test scores or other modes of assessment" (1989b, 5). In this definition, there are two striking differences from traditional notions of validity. First of all, Messick includes multiple theoretical as well as empirical considerations. In other words, in writing assessment, the validity of a test must include a recognizable and supportable theoretical foundation as well as empirical data from students' work. Second, a test's validity also includes its use. Decisions based upon a test that, for example, is used for purposes outside a relevant theoretical foundation for the teaching of writing would have a low, unacceptable degree of validity. Cronbach's stance is similar. For Cronbach validity "must link concepts, evidence, social and personal consequences, and values" (1988, 4).

In both of these definitions of validity, we are asked to consider more than just empirical or technical aspects of the way we assess. In writing assessment, the technical aspects of creating rubrics, training raters, developing writing prompts, and the like have been the reasons why outside objective measures were superior to just having teachers read and make specific judgments about student writers. These new conceptions of validity question our preoccupation with the technical aspects of writing assessment procedures. In Cronbach's terms, we will need to link together these technical features with what we know about writing and the teaching of writing. In addition to establishing and expanding the theoretical and empirical foundation for assessing writing, both Messick and Cronbach's definitions require us to establish a theoretical foundation for the way we assess and to ensure that the evaluation of writing only be used for educational purposes which encourage the teaching and learning of writing.

Few important or long lasting changes can occur in the way we assess student writing outside of the classroom unless we attempt to change the theory which drives our practices and attitudes toward assessment. At present, assessment procedures that attempt to fix objectively a student's ability to write are based upon an outdated theory supported by an irrelevant epistemology. Emergent ideas about measurement define teaching, learning, and assessment in new ways, ways that are compatible with our own developing theories about literacy, though for the most part they have yet to filter down to the assessment of student writing. The result has been a stalemate for writing assessment. Although we were able to move from single-sample impromptu essays to portfolios in less than thirty years, we are still primarily concerned with constructing scoring guidelines and achieving high levels of interrater reliability.

EXAMINING AND UNDERSTANDING NEW PROCEDURES

This section explores our ability to construct a theory of writing assessment based upon our understandings about the nature of language, written communication, and its teaching. The bases for this theoretical exploration are current practices at universities who have been using assessment procedures unsupported by conventional writing assessment's reliance on the positivist, epistemological foundations of classical test theory. These new procedures recognize the importance of context, rhetoric, and other characteristics integral to a specific purpose and institution. The procedures are site-based, practical, and have been developed and controlled locally. They were created by faculty and administrators at individual institutions to solve specific assessment needs and to address particular problems. Individually, these procedures for assessing writing provide solutions for specific institutions. It is my hope to connect these procedures through their common sets of beliefs and assumptions to create the possibility of a theoretical umbrella. This theorizing can help other institutions create their own procedures that solve local assessment problems and recognize the importance of context, rhetoric, teaching, and learning. By themselves, each of these institutions has had to develop and create its own wheel; together, they can aid others in understanding the nature of their assessment needs and to provide solutions that "link together" the concerns of a variety of stakeholders.[3]

One of the most common forms of writing assessment employed by many institutions is the placement of students into various writing courses offered by a specific college or university. Traditionally, schools have used holistic scoring procedures to place students, adapting specific numerical scores, usually the combined or sum scores of two raters, to indicate placement for a particular class. Some of the earliest and most interesting procedures developed outside the traditional theoretical umbrella for writing assessment involve placement. Current traditional placement procedures require the additional steps necessary to code rater decisions numerically and to apply these numbers to specific courses. Research indicates that traditional procedures might be even more indirect, since talk-aloud protocols of raters using holistic methods for placement demonstrate that raters often first decide on student placement into a class and then locate the appropriate numerical score that reflects their decision (Huot 1993; Pula and Huot 1993). Newer placement programs end this indirection by having raters make placement decisions directly.

The first and most rigorously documented of the new placement programs was developed by William L. Smith (1993) at the University of Pittsburgh. His method involved using instructors to place students in specific classes based upon the writing ability necessary for success in the courses those instructors actually taught. This method of placing students proved to be more cost-efficient and effective than conventional scoring methods (Smith 1993). Such a placement program circumvents many of the problems found in current placement testing. Raters are hired in groups of two to represent each of the courses in which students can be placed. These pairs of raters are chosen because their most immediate and extensive teaching experience is in a specific course. A rater either decides that a student belongs in her class or passes the paper on to the rater for the class in which she thinks the student belongs. Using standard holistic scoring methods to verify this contextual placement scoring procedure, Smith found that students were placed into courses with greater teacher satisfaction and without the need for rubrics, training sessions, quantification, and interrater reliability.

While this method has been revised as the curriculum it supports is also revised (Harris 1996), these changes are in keeping with the local nature of this and other emergent writing assessment methods. Unlike traditional methods that centralize rating guidelines or other features of an assessment scheme, these site-based procedures can and should be constantly revised to meet the developing needs of an institution. For my purposes in this chapter, Smith's (1993) or other procedures that have been developed outside of a psychometric framework are less important for the utilization of the procedures themselves and more for their ability to define a set of principles capable of solving particular assessment problems, developed and revised according to local assessment needs.[4]

Another placement procedure, dubbed a two-tier process, has been developed at Washington State University, in which student essays are read by a single reader who makes one decision about whether or not students should enter the most heavily enrolled first-year composition course (Haswell and Wyche-Smith 1994). Students not so placed by the first-tier reader have their essays read in mutual consultation by a second tier of raters, experts in all courses in the curriculum. In this method, sixty percent of all students are placed into a course on the first reading. [5]

Pedagogically, these contextualized forms of placement assessment are sound because teachers make placement decisions based upon what they know about writing and the curriculum of the courses they teach. Placement of students in various levels of composition instruction is primarily a teaching decision. Smith (1993) analyzed the talk-aloud protocols of his raters and found that they made placement decisions upon whether or not they could "see" a particular student in their classrooms. Judith Pula and I (1993) report similar findings from interviewing raters reading placement essays in holistic scoring sessions. Raters reported making placement decisions not upon the established scoring guidelines on a numerical rubric but rather on the "teachability" of students. The context for reading student writing appears to guide raters regardless of rubrics or training found in many assessment practices (Huot 1993; Pula and Huot 1993).

While the first two procedures I've discussed have to do with placement, the others involve exit exams and program assessment. Michael Allen (1995) discusses his and his colleagues' experience with reading portfolios from various institutions. Allen found that readers who knew the context and institutional guidelines of the school at which the portfolios were written could achieve an acceptable rate of interrater reliability by just discussing the essays on-line over the internet, without any need for scoring guidelines or training sessions. Allen theorizes that readers are able "to put on the hat" of other institutions because they are experts in reading student writing and teaching student writers.

While Allen (1995) discusses the results and implications of reading program portfolios with a group of teachers across the country, Durst, Roemer, and Schultz (1994) write about using portfolios read by a team of teachers as an exit exam at the University of Cincinnati to determine whether or not students should move from one course to another. What makes their system different is that these "trios," as the three-teacher teams are called, not only read each others' portfolios but discuss that work to make "internal struggles [about value and judgment] outward and visible" (286). This system revolves around the notion that talk is integral to understanding the value of a given student portfolio. While White (1994) and Elbow and Belanoff (1986) have noted that bringing teachers together to talk about standards and values was one of the most important aspects of writing assessment, Durst, Roemer, and Schultz (1994) make the conversation between teachers the center of their portfolio exit scheme. They assert that their system for exit examination has benefits beyond the accurate assessment of student writing: "portfolio negotiations can serve as an important means of faculty development, can help ease anxieties about grading and passing judgment on students' work, and can provide a forum for teachers and administrators to rethink the goals of a freshman English program" (287). This public discussion of student work not only furnishes a workable method to determine the exit of particular students but also provides real benefits for the teachers and curriculum at a specific institution as newer conceptions of validity advocate (Cronbach 1988; 1989; Messick 1989a; 1989b; Moss 1992).

While all of the methods we have examined have distinctions predicated upon the context of their role(s) for a specific institution or purpose, they also share assumptions about the importance of situating assessment methods and rater judgment within a particular rhetorical, linguistic and pedagogical context. The focus of each of these programs is inward toward the needs of students, teachers and programs rather than outward toward standardized norms or generalizable criteria. In sharp contrast to the acontextual assumptions of traditional procedures (see figure one), these developing methods depend on specific assessment situations and contexts. Figure two summarizes the procedures and purposes of these emergent assessment methods.

IMPACT ON RELIABILITY

All of the procedures and the assumptions they hold either bypass or make moot the most important feature of current traditional writing assessment—the agreement of independent readers, or interrater reliability. Although Smith's (1993) procedures involve raters reading independently (without discussion or collaboration), rater agreement, by itself, is not crucial,

Figure 2

New, Emergent Writing Assessment
Procedures, Purposes and Assumptions

PROCEDURE	PURPOSE	ASSUMPTIONS
raters from specific courses place students into their courses	writing placement	placement is a teaching decision based on specific curricular knowledge
one rater reads all essays and places 60% of all students; other 40% placed by expert team of consultants	writing placement	placement largely a screening process; teachers recognize students in primary course
rater groups discuss portfolios for exit or specific level of achievement	exit and program assessment	discussion and multiple interpretation necessary for high stakes decisions about students or programs
validity	determine accuracy assessment and impact of process on teaching and learning for a specific site and its mission and goals	value of an assessment can only be known and accountable to a specific context

because all raters are not equally good judges for all courses. Those decisions by the teachers of the course are privileged, since they are made by the experts for that course and that educational decision.

One of the possible reasons why we have historically needed methods to ensure rater agreement stems from the stripping away of context, common in conventional writing assessment procedures to obtain objective and consistent scores. This absence of context distorts the ability of individuals who rely on it to make meaning. For example, the most famous study involving the inability of raters to agree on scores for the same papers conducted by Paul Diederich, John French, and Sydell Carlton (1961) gave readers no sense of where the papers came from or the purpose of the reading. Given the total lack of context within which these papers were read, it is not surprising that they were scored without consistency. The absence of context in traditional writing assessment procedures could be responsible for the lack of agreement among raters that these procedures, ironically, are supposed to supply. The traditional response to raters' inability to agree has been to impose an artificial context, consisting of scoring guidelines and rater training in an attempt to "calibrate" human judges as one might adjust a mechanical tool, instrument or machine. White (1994) and other early advocates of holistic and other current traditional procedures for evaluating writing likened these scoring sessions to the creation of a discourse community of readers. However, Pula's and my (1993) study of the influence of teacher experience, training, and personal background on raters outlines the existence of two discourse communities in a holistic scoring session: one, the immediate group of raters, and the other, a community whose membership depends upon disciplinary, experiential and social ties. It seems practically and theoretically sound that we design schemes for assessment on the second discourse community instead of attempting to superimpose one just for assessment purposes.

Clearly, this inability of raters to agree in contextually stripped environments has fueled the overwhelming emphasis on reliability in writing assessment. Michael Williamson (1994) examines the connection between reliability and validity in writing assessment by looking at the ways more reliable measures like multiple-choice exams are actually less valid for evaluating student writing. Looking at validity and reliability historically, Williamson concludes that "the properties of a test which establish its reliability do not necessarily contribute to its validity" (1994, 162). Williamson goes on to challenge the traditional notion that reliability is a precondition for validity: "Thus, comparatively high reliability is neither a necessary nor a sufficient condition for establishing the validity of a measure" (1994, 162).

While Williamson contends that reliability should be just one aspect of judging the worthwhile nature of an assessment, Pamela Moss (1994) asks the question in her title, "Can There be Validity Without Reliability?" Moss asserts that reliability in the psychometric sense "requires a significant level of standardization [and that] this privileging of standardization is problematic" (1994, 6). Moss goes on to explore what assessment procedures look like within a hermeneutic framework. She uses the example of a faculty search in which members of a committee read an entire dossier of material from prospective candidates and make hiring decisions only after a full discussion with other members of the committee. In a later article, Moss (1996) explores the value of drawing on the work and procedures from interpretive research traditions to increase an understanding of the importance of context in assessment. Instead of interchangeable consistency within an interpretive tradition, reliability becomes a critical standard with which communities of knowledgeable stakeholders make important and valid decisions.

Interpretive research traditions like hermeneutics support the emerging procedures in writing evaluation because they "privilege interpretations from readers most knowledgeable about the context of assessment" (Moss 1994a, 9). An interpretive framework supports the linguistic context within which all writing assessment should take place, because it acknowledges the indeterminacy of meaning and the importance of individual and communal interpretations and values. Interpretive research traditions hold special significance for the assessment of student writing, since reading and writing are essentially interpretive acts. It is a truism in current ideas about literacy that context is a critical component in the ability of people to transact meaning with written language. In composition pedagogy, we have been concerned with creating meaningful contexts in which students write. A theory of assessment that recognizes the importance of context should also be concerned with creating assessment procedures that establish meaningful contexts within which teachers read and assess. Building a context in which writing can be drafted, read, and evaluated is a step toward the creation of assessment practices based on recognizable characteristics of language use. Assessment procedures that ignore or attempt to overcome context distort the communicative situation. Michael Halliday asserts that "Any account of language which fails to build in the situation as an essential ingredient is likely to be artificial and unrewarding" (1978, 29). Halliday's contention that "*All* language functions in contexts of situations and is relatable to those contexts" (1978, 32) is part of a consensus among scholars in sociolinguistics (Labov 1980), pragmatics (Levinson 1983), discourse analysis (Brown and Yule 1983), and text linguistics (de Beaugrande and Dressler 1981) about the preeminence of context in language use.

CREATING NEW ASSESSMENTS OF WRITING

Research on the nature of raters' decisions (Barritt, Stock and Clark 1986; Pula and Huot 1993) indicate the powerful tension teachers feel between their roles as readers and raters in an assessment environment. An appropriate way to harness this tension is to base assessment practices within specific contexts, so that raters are forced to make practical, pedagogical, programmatic, and interpretive judgments without having to define writing quality or other abstract values which end up tapping influences beyond the raters or test administrators' control. As Smith (1993) and Haswell and Wyche-Smith (1994) have illustrated with placement readers, Durst, Roemer, and Schultz (1994) with exit raters, and Allen (1995) with program assessment, we can harness the expertise and ability of raters within the place they know, live, work and read. Assessment practices need to be based upon the notion that we are attempting to assess a writer's ability to communicate within a particular context and to a specific audience who needs to read this writing as part of a clearly defined communicative event.

It follows logically and theoretically that rather than base assessment decisions on the abstract and inaccurate notion of writing quality as a fixed entity[6]—a notion which is driven by a positivist view of reality—we should define each evaluative situation and judge students upon their ability to accomplish a specific communicative task, much like the basic tenets of primary trait scoring. However, instead of just basing the scores upon rhetorical principles, I propose that we design the complete assessment procedure upon the purpose and context of the specific writing ability to be described and evaluated. The three major means for assessing writing, holistic, analytic and primary trait, are largely text-based procedures which merely manipulate the numerically-based scoring guidelines. These procedures would be replaced by contextually and rhetorically defined testing environments. The type of scoring would be identified by the genre of the text to be written, the discipline within which it was produced and the type of decisions the raters are attempting to make.

In business writing, for example, students might be required to condense extensive documents into a few paragraphs for an executive summary. Students in the natural or physical sciences might be given the data obtained through research procedures and be required to present such information in a recognizable format, complete with applications. In environmental writing, where speed and the ability to synthesize technical information for a lay audience is crucial, students might be given a prompt they have never seen and be asked to produce text in a relatively short period of time. Instead of current methods, we would have placement testing for first-year composition or business competency writing or high school exit writing in which the purpose, context and criteria would be linked together to create procedures built upon the rhetorical, linguistic, practical and pedagogical demands of reading and writing in a specific context. Debates, for example, about the use of single-samples or portfolios (Purves 1995; White 1995a; 1995b), would be moot, since the number and type of writing samples and the method for producing the texts would depend upon the specific assessment context. The criteria for judgment would be built into a method and purpose for assessment and would be available, along with successful examples of such writing to the student writers. Not only do these proposed methods for assessing writing reject scoring guidelines, rater training for agreement, calculations of interrater reliability, and the other technologies of testing, but they also connect the context, genre, and discipline of the writing with those making evaluative decisions and the criteria they use to judge this writing. When we begin to base writing evaluation on the context of a specific rhetorical situation adjudged by experts from within a particular area, we can eliminate the guessing students now go through in preparing for such examinations, as well as the abstract debates and considerations about the best procedures for a wide variety of assessment purposes.

TOWARD A NEW THEORY OF WRITING ASSESSMENT

The proposed writing assessments we have discussed and other procedures like them exist outside the "old" theoretical tenets of classical test theory.[7] Instead of generalizability, technical rigor and large scale measures that minimize context and aim for a standardization of writing quality, these new procedures emphasize the context of the texts being read, the position of the readers and the local, practical standards that teachers and other stakeholders hold for written communication. There is a clear link between the judgments being made and the outcome of these judgments that is neither hidden nor shaded by reference to numerical scores, guidelines or statistical calculations of validity or reliability. These site-based, locally-driven procedures for evaluating student writing have their roots in the methods and beliefs held by the teachers who teach the courses that students are entering or exiting, or in the program under review. In this light, there is a much clearer connection between the way writing is taught and the way it is evaluated. For the last two or three decades, writing pedagogy has moved toward process-oriented and context-specific approaches that focus on students' individual cognitive energies and their socially positioned identities as members of culturally bound groups. In contrast, writing assessment has remained a contextless activity emphasizing standardization and an ideal version of writing quality.

These emergent methods can be viewed under a new theoretical umbrella, one supported by evolving conceptions of validity that include the consequences of the tests and a linking of instruction and practical purposes with the concept of measuring students' ability to engage in a specific literacy event or events. These procedures also have their bases in theories of language and literacy that recognize the importance of context and the individual in constructing acceptable written communication. These methods are sensitive to the importance of interpretation inherent in transactional and psycholinguistic theories of reading. Although it is premature to attempt any overall or complete discussion of the criteria for newer conceptions of writing assessment, figure three provides a set of preliminary principles extrapolated from our consideration and discussion of these new assessment procedures and their connection to current theories of measurement, language, and composition pedagogy. Like the assessment practices themselves, any writing assessment theory will need to be considered a work in progress as new procedures and the theories that inform them continue to advance our theoretical and practical understanding of writing assessment.

Figure 3

Principles For a New Theory
And Practice of Writing Assessment

Site-Based

An assessment for writing is developed in response to a specific need that occurs at a specific site. Procedures are based upon the resources and concerns of an institution, department, program or agency and its administrators, faculty, students or other constituents.

Locally-Controlled

The individual institution or agency is responsible for managing, revising, updating and validating the assessment procedures, which should in turn be carefully reviewed according to clearly outlined goals and guidelines on a regular basis to safeguard the concerns of all those affected by the assessment process.

Context-Sensitive

The procedures should honor the instructional goals and objectives as well as the cultural and social environment of the institution or agency and its students, teachers and other stakeholders. It is important to establish and maintain the contextual integrity necessary for the authentic reading and writing of textual communication.

Rhetorically-Based

All writing assignments, scoring criteria, writing environments and reading procedures should adhere to recognizable and supportable rhetorical principles integral to the thoughtful expression and reflective interpretation of texts.

Accessible

All procedures and rationales for the creation of writing assignments, scoring criteria and reading procedures, as well as samples of student work and rater judgment, should be available to those whose work is being evaluated.

Developing writing assessment procedures upon an epistemological basis that honors local standards, includes a specific context for both the composing and reading of student writing and allows the communal interpretation of written communication is an important first step in furnishing a new theoretical umbrella for assessing student writing. However, it is only a first step. We must also develop procedures with which to document and validate their use. These validation procedures must be sensitive to the local and contextual nature of the procedures themselves. While traditional writing assessment methods rely on statistical validation and standardization that are important to the beliefs and assumptions that fuel them, developing procedures will need to employ more qualitative and ethnographic validation procedures like interviews, observations and thick descriptions to understand the role an assessment plays within a specific program or institution. We can also study course outcomes to examine specific assessments based upon specific curricula. William L. Smith's (1993) validation procedures at the University of Pittsburgh and Richard Haswell's (2001) at Washington State can probably serve as models for documenting emerging procedures.

These local procedures can be connected beyond a specific context by public displays of student work and locally developed standards. Harold Berlak (1992) proposes that the use of samples from several locations be submitted to a larger board of reviewers who represent individual localities and that this larger board conduct regular reviews of student work and individual assessment programs. Pamela Moss (1994a) outlines a model in which representative samples of student work and localized assessment procedures work can be reviewed by outside agencies. Allen's (1995) study furnishes a model for a "board" of expert readers from across the country to examine specific assessment programs, including samples of student work and the local judgments given that work.[8] His use of electronic communication points out the vast potential the Internet and the Web have in providing the linkage and access necessary to connect site-based, locally controlled assessment programs from various locations. As Moss

(1994a) cautions, we have only begun to revise a very established measurement mechanism, and there is much we still need to learn about how to set up, validate and connect local assessment procedures.

It is important to note that all of the procedures I have highlighted as depending upon an emergent theory of assessment that recognize context and local control were developed at the college level. Even state-mandated portfolio systems like those in Kentucky and Vermont continue to be standardized in order to provide for acceptable rates of interrater reliability. It is imperative that we at the college level continue our experimentation and expand our theorizing to create a strong platform for new writing assessment theory and practice. Connecting those who work in college writing assessment with those engaged in writing assessment from the educational measurement community, as I advocate in chapter two, can not only foster a more unified field but can also provide the possibility of rhetorical and contextual writing assessment for all students. We need to begin thinking of writing evaluation not so much as the ability to judge accurately a piece of writing or a particular writer, but as the ability to describe the promise and limitations of a writer working within a particular rhetorical and linguistic context.

As much as these new procedures for writing assessment might make practical and theoretical sense to those of us who teach and research written communication, they will not be widely developed or implemented without much work and struggle, without an increased emphasis on writing assessment within the teaching of writing at all levels. English teachers' justifiable distrust of writing assessment has given those without knowledge and appreciation of literacy and its teaching the power to assess our students. The ability to assess is the ability to determine and control what is valuable. Standardized forms of assessment locate the power for making decisions about students with a central authority. Harold Berlak (1992) labels the educational policies of the Reagan-Bush era "incoherent," because while policy makers called for increased local control of schools, they also instituted

massive standardized testing, rendering any kind of local decision-making superfluous. Changing the foundation that directs
the way student writing is assessed involves altering the power
relations between students and teachers, and teachers and
administrators. It can also change what we will come to value as
literacy in and outside of school. At this point, the door is open
for real and lasting changes in writing assessment procedures. We
who teach and research written communication need to become
active in assessment issues and active developers of these new,
emergent practices. In the past, current writing assessment procedures were largely developed by ETS and other testing companies outside of a community of English or composition teachers
and were based upon a set of assumptions and beliefs irrelevant
to written communication. Unlike the past, it is time for us to go
through the door and take charge of how our students are to be
evaluated. It is time to build and maintain writing assessment theories and practices which are consonant with our teaching and
research.

5

READING LIKE A TEACHER
Toward a Theory of Response

Like chapter three, this chapter focuses on activities in the writing classroom and is concerned with the way our evaluation of and response to students' writing affects their ability to learn. As I have in all the chapters in this volume, I start here with what we currently know or perceive about a specific component of assessing student writing and attempt to re-articulate it in ways that can further promote teaching and learning. My study of and ideas about response have been evolving over the last decade or so. For example, I regularly teach a doctoral seminar on writing assessment called "Assessing and Responding to Student Writing," and I include a responding-to-student-writing section in both of my teaching writing courses, one for high school teachers and one for those teaching at the college level. The evolution of activities and readings I have used in courses like these to prepare teachers to respond to student writing has been an important experience for my own evolving thought about response practices. This chapter reflects my continuing struggle to understand and improve my own response practices, along with those of the teachers I work with, and to say something important about the act of responding to student writing. All of these experiences and activities have lead me to the conclusion that we currently lack a sufficient theory for responding to student writing. Although no single chapter could possibly articulate a coherent theory of response, I explore the theoretical soundness of the ways we respond to student writers and teach new instructors to respond. My goal is to unearth the beliefs and assumptions that guide current response practices and hold a critical eye toward them and the act of responding to student writing. This practical, grounded notion of theory rooted in the ideas of James Zebroski (1994) and Louise Phelps (1989; 1998; 2000) attempts throughout the volume to blur distinctions between theory and practice in writing assessment, creating a more conscious awareness of where our practices come from and how we can use them to promote teaching and learning.

More than twenty years ago, Nancy Sommers (1982) told us what we already knew but were afraid to acknowledge—that teachers' written comments were more concerned with students' ability to write correctly than to make any kind of meaning. Robert Connors and Andrea Lunsford's (1993) study of almost three thousand student papers revealed much the same. Anthologies published about ten years ago (Anson 1989; Lawson, Sterr, Ryan, and Winterowd 1989) provided alternative ways of responding to student writing, and attempted to foreground discussions of teacher response in how we read, interpret and make meaning of written communication. The focus of most response literature is on different ways we can respond to student writing, on practice rather than theory. More recently, Richard Straub (1996; 1997; 2000) has conducted a series of studies on response, most of which document the different ways in which certain teachers can read the same students' writing. In one essay on response, Straub (2000) examines his own responding practices in light of seven principles he extrapolates from the research on response: 1) "Turn your comments into a conversation" (28); 2) "Do not take control over a student's text" (31); 3) "Give priority to global concerns of content, organization and purpose before getting (overly) involved with style and correctness" (34); 4) "Limit the scope of your comments and the number of comments you present" (40); 5) "Select your focus of comments according to the stage of drafting and relative maturity of the text" (40): 6) "Gear your comments to the individual student" (42). 7) "Make frequent use of praise" (46). While I find little to disagree with in the principles Straub advocates, I see little advancement in such principles for an overall understanding of teacher response. Instead, the focus is once again only on practice, with little attempt to see response within a theoretical, pedagogical, or communicative context. (For a more thorough treatment of Straub's work, see Murphy 2000 and Phelps 2000.) What's also important to note is that all of Straub's principles focus exclusively on the writing of comments without any attention to the teacher's reading of student writing.

One of the reasons the literature on responding to student writing has focused on methods for response is that many of us are unhappy with more traditional methods for responding to student writing. As well, it is difficult not to hold negative views about the way teachers read student writing, considering studies like those conducted by Nancy Sommers (1982) and Robert Connors and Andrea Lunsford (1993). In her book chapter, "Reading Like a Teacher and Teaching Like a Reader," Virginia Chappell (1991) defines what I take to be some rather widely held notions about what reading like a teacher means to many of us: "That mythology includes what I call reading like a teacher: the fault-finding summative evaluation of student writing that makes grades, their bestowal and their receipt, so distasteful" (55). Chappell goes on to illustrate why teachers' readings are held in suspicion and distaste: "But as we know, teachers tend to read students' texts to evaluate them, and, as William Irmscher has pointed out, teachers tend to evaluate by finding fault (148)" (59). Edward White (1995) and Peter Elbow (1991) both have written about how we cannot trust teachers' evaluations, with White advocating the use of holistic scoring as a way to control teacher's inconsistencies.

In her chapter on responding to student writing, Louise Phelps (1989) includes this negative notion of reading in her first category of teacher response, "Evaluative Attitude, Closed Text" (49) in which a teacher grades a stack or set of student papers. Lil Brannon and Cy Knoblauch (1982) describe response of this type by noting that instructors often compare student writing to an ideal text. Phelps is accurate in describing the status of scholarship on response: "Yet today's study of response remains a minor subspecialization pursued by a relatively small group of scholars, rather than the central theoretical concern for the discipline."(2000, 92). Richard Miller's point mentioned in chapter three bears repeating here: "learning how to solicit, read, and respond to the reading and writing done by the student populace—those people who stand inside and outside the academy simultaneously—has been and continues to be the most pressing challenge confronting those who work in English Studies" (1994, 179). Unfortunately, there has, for the most part, been little attention to the theory and practice of responding to student writers. Instead, we have focused on various ways to respond—or have attempted to isolate and study the ways different teachers might respond—to the same student. Jane Mathison Fife and Peggy O'Neill (2001) tell us that whether the scholarship looks at the response practices of a range of teachers or focuses on individuals, these studies for the most part are conducted outside of any pedagogical context.

My attempt to rearticulate what it means to read like a teacher hopes to create, in Phelps's (1989) terms, a dialectic between the way we think about language and teaching and the way we read and respond to student writing. This dialectic questions a continued focus on methods for response and on studies of teacher response outside of the context of teaching writing, just as it questions a continuing suspicion of teachers' response. A dialectic between theory and practice shifts the focus from *how* we respond to *why* we respond, making us reflect upon and articulate our beliefs and assumptions about literacy and its teaching. It is time for the profession to reconceptualize its approach to evaluating and responding to student writing. Instead of just developing alternative methods for couching our commentary, we need to come to an understanding of where our comments come from. What are the constraints teachers work under when they read student writing? What are the occasions for responding? What is a teacher doing when she reads, and what affects her ability to make meaning and assign value?

Before we can begin to answer such questions (and surely a cogent response to all of them is beyond the scope of a single chapter), let us start with a question we can answer. Why do teachers read student writing in the first place? Ostensibly, we read student writing to teach student writers: "In fact, pedagogical purpose saturates the whole phenomenon of response" (Phelps 2000, 101). It follows, then, that reading like a teacher means reading to teach. As Phelps points out, making a teaching move can be different than just responding to a text, and it might also be noted that in Connors and Lunsford's (1993) study of teacher commentary, over sixty percent of the comments in the study focused on justifying teachers grades, so while it may be fair to say that overall teachers read student writing to teach student writers, at times this overall goal can become short-circuited. Nonetheless, my approach to teacher response is to start with the teacher's attempt to use feedback to the writer as a pedagogical device. As with most other techniques used in the writing classroom, teacher commentary should be used to foster writing skills in our students. This claim for the pedagogical value of teacher commentary must be rooted in the contextual nature of language teaching and learning within a curriculum dependent upon abilities learned through practice—as in a classroom where students learn to write by writing. In other words, we can only judge teacher commentary based upon its ability to help a particular student become a better writer within a specific educational context. Rather than categorizing teachers' methods of response, or developing certain principles, it is time we began to study the dynamics of reading student writing, to know what it means to read and respond like a teacher.

THEORIES OF READING AND RESPONSE

I begin with a rather obvious point: to assess student writing, we have to read it first. As Louise Phelps notes, "Response is fundamentally reading, not writing" (2000, 93). Any constraints attached to the process of reading, therefore, are also constraints on the process of evaluating student writing. In other words, we are limited in our ability to evaluate student writing by the process we use to make meaning of text in the first place. Whether we look at a portfolio, write on papers or via email, speak into a tape recorder or speak with students in or outside of our offices or over the telephone, we must first read the student's paper. No matter what else we do with the writing after we receive it, we are constrained by the very process of reading. It follows that information about reading is information about responding to and assessing student writing.

Reading is a dynamic, meaning-making activity that revolves around the individual reader's attempt to understand and interpret what has been written. The meaning anyone makes of a given text depends upon her prior background, training, experience and expectations. As Frank Smith (1982) points out, "In a sense, information already available in the brain is more important in reading than information available to the eyes from the print on the page, even when the text is quite new and unfamiliar" (9). In this light, teachers' previous experience with students and their texts adds to and controls their ability not only to respond but to devise meaning from the text itself. Even the very role of teacher can affect the kind of reading given by an individual. Peter Elbow (1973) has noted the different kinds of meaning readers can derive from text depending upon whether or not they play the "doubting game" or "believing game." Robert Tierney and P. David Pearson (1983) coined the term "alignment" to describe the different points of view from which a reader constructs a text while reading: "We see alignment as having two facets: stances a reader or writer assumes in collaboration with their author or audience and roles within which the reader or writer immerse themselves as they proceed with the topic" (572). Tierney and Pearson go on to cite research that shows that differing alignments can affect the quantity and nature of what a reader remembers from a particular text. This concept of alignment as an individual phenomenon can also be extended to the notion of the interpretive community. Stanley Fish (1980) contends that an interpretive community also affects what a reader can see within a text: "What I am suggesting is that an interpretive entity, endowed with purposes and concern, is, by virtue of its very operation, determining what counts as the facts to be observed" (8).

In his book chapter "A Hero in the Classroom" James Zebroski (1989) illustrates Fish's point about the way certain theoretical orientations can affect the way we read student writing. Zebroski includes one of his students' essays in his chapter and offers four different responses based on the different ways in which he might read this student's work—what Zebroski calls the different voices he hears when reading this particular essay. One response is through the voice of a pop grammarian whom Zebroski labels "Simon Newman," in which Zebroski focuses exclusively on the errors the student makes and finds the essay completely unacceptable, calling for the student to go back to the basics. The second response is from the new critical perspective of "John Crowe Redemption," in which the reading focuses on structure and how it relates to meaning. This response calls for the student to begin anew in the middle of the essay, in order to produce a more structurally consistent piece of writing. The third response is from "Mina Flaherty" who focuses on the logic of the writer's choices, referring to him by name and pointing out to the first two responders that "Dave" does many things right and that he would profit from instruction about audience and other rhetorical matters. The last response and clearly the one most favored by Zebroski is from "Mikhail Zebroski Bakhtin" which focuses on the intertextuality of the writing, looking for the connections between the writer's ideas and the sources for his sense of reality. This reading traces Dave's understanding about power relations and his position in a politically-charged world. In Fish's terms, and through Zebroski's example, it's fairly clear that the type of reading given by an individual reader actually controls what that reader can observe within a text. This control of observation as it relates to the reading of teachers is beautifully illustrated in Joseph Williams's (1981) article, "The Phenomenology of Error" where the reader (usually an English teacher) fails to note the multitude of errors within a piece of writing because she is not looking for them.

She is reading in her role as professional colleague, and she assumes and therefore receives mechanical correctness, whether it is in the text or not, from an author she believes to be an authority.

Arnetha Ball's (1997) study exploring and comparing African American teachers' and Euro American teachers' responses to an ethnically mixed group of students is one of the few examples we have of the ways in which ethnic diversity can impact teacher response. Ball had two sets of teachers, Euro American and African American, read essays from three different groups of students: Euro American, African American and Hispanic American. She found that the Euro American teachers rated the Euro American students highest in overall writing quality with a mean score of 5.06 on a six point scale; African American students were rated 3.98, and Hispanic American Students 2.97 (175). African American teachers, on the other hand, rated Euro American students at 3.31, African American Students at 3.35, and Hispanic students at 2.85 (175). The clear progression of writing quality perceived by Euro American teachers, with Euro American students on top and African American and Hispanic American students one point consecutively below, disappears according to African American teachers. In contrast, they perceive Euro and African American students as about the same and Hispanic American students about a half a point below. Clearly, "writing quality" in this instance is a feature influenced by cultural identity.

The influence of culture seems even stronger when we look at Ball's teachers' scores for students' use of mechanics (sentence boundaries, agreement and spelling). Euro American teachers' mean scores for mechanics for Euro American students was 3.63 on a four point scale (175). For African American students it was 2.82, and it was 2.22 for Hispanic American students (175). These sets of scores for mechanics seem to follow the pattern that Euro American teachers displayed for overall writing quality, since African American students were ranked .8 behind Euro American students with Hispanic American students 1.4 behind Euro American and .6 behind African American students (175). While these differences appear not quite as marked numerically as the ones for overall writing quality, it should be noted that they are closer than they seem, since mechanics was rated on a four point scale rather than the six point scale used for overall writing quality.

African American teachers' perception of correctness in student writing follows the pattern of difference from Euro American teachers for overall writing quality, but, even more so. African American teachers overall score for Euro American student's mechanics was 2.19 (175), a full point and a half lower on a four point scale than Euro American teachers. African American students scored higher but not much at 2.34, a half point lower than the Euro American teachers, and Hispanic American students scored 2.03, almost two tenths of a point lower than the Euro American teachers. What's interesting in the African American teachers' scores is that they are lower than the ones given by Euro American teachers and that for mechanics, all three groups of students are clustered together within three tenths of a point. In this case, teachers with different cultural orientations saw very different things in student writing.

It's important in talking about the influence of culture in teacher response that we not forget that school itself is a cultural system bound by specific beliefs and attitudes. For example, Sarah Freedman (1984) demonstrated that teachers' perceptions of writing quality were tied to the roles they expect students to assume when writing in a school-sponsored situation. Freedman used a holistic scoring session to include five essays written by professional writers. These essays were judged by the teacher-scorers, trained as holistic raters, to be inferior to student written essays. Freedman noted that the professionally-written essay violated norms associated with student writing: "they were threateningly familiar, some defied the task, they wrote too definitely about novel ideas, and they displayed a literally unbelievable amount of knowledge" (1984, 344). Reading within their roles as teachers, then, these raters judged such writing as inappropriate for student writers.

Lester Faigley's essay "Judging Writers Judging Selves" (1989) discusses the ways in which teacher/evaluators come to assess the value of student writing. Faigley isolates two moments in time, one in the 1930s and one in the 1980s. He examines evaluations of two essays written in 1929 that were included as part of an external review of the College Entrance Examination's Board by a nine-member Commission on English in the 1930s. Faigley discusses the obvious importance of a canonical knowledge of literature and the more academic approach adopted by one of the students versus the use of popular fiction by another writer. Faigley is convincing in his portrayal of the importance of a certain type of cultural knowledge being privileged in the assessments given by both the college board and the external review. Faigley's second moment focuses on an anthology of student writing prepared in 1985, in which composition teachers from across the country were asked to submit examples of the best student writing they had received. Almost all of the student essays were personal narratives, and the discussion of student writing focused on such qualities as how authentic and truthful they were. Faigley's point is that our evaluations of student work are often connected to our sense of value. For example, in the 1930s, teachers valued certain canonical knowledge, whereas in the 1980s, teacher focus was on personal disclosure and its ability to display authentic or truthful human experience. He concludes his essay with a writing sample about a young woman's experience in Paris to highlight how the familiar and valued influence our sense of quality in student writing. Culture and privilege continue to evolve and be marked in different ways, and teachers' reading of student writing is continuously influenced by their cultured sense of value.

One last element important to an understanding of how the process of reading can affect the reading done by teachers is expectation. Since teachers can expect different texts from different students and different assignments or writing situations, expectation should not be considered a constant. Wolfgang Iser (1978) in his book, *The Act of Reading*, coins the term "wandering viewpoint" to describe the flexible nature of the reader's expectations in her ability to comprehend written discourse. As Susan Sulieman (1980) points out, expectation, a powerful force in the mind's ability to anticipate textual clues and construct meaning, can be altered by a variety of factors connected with and even within a particular reading. For example, a teacher would have very different expectations for a first draft than she would for a piece of writing she had already read and commented upon.

So powerful is rater expectation that Paul Diederich (1974) notes that raters score the same essays higher when they were designated as coming from an honors class, and Leo Rigsby (1987) reports significantly higher scores for essays known to be from upper classmen in departmental competency exams. Patricia Stock and Jay Robinson (1987) contend that rater expectation may be as important as the student text itself in determining scores received in direct writing assessment. Because reader expectation is based upon prior experience, it is one of the basic ingredients in the fluent reading process.

It is important for us to understand that reading and responding to student writing constitutes a particular kind of literacy event. For example, Connors and Lunsford (1993) compare the number of errors marked by readers in the 1980s with the number of errors marked by readers in studies done in 1917 and 1930. They sum up their findings in this way:

> Finally, we feel we can report some good news. One very telling fact emerging from our research is our realization that college students are not making more formal errors than they used to. The numbers of errors made by students in earlier studies and the numbers we found in the 1980s agree remarkably . . . The consistency of these numbers seems to us extraordinary. It suggests that although the length of the average paper demanded in freshman composition has been steadily rising, the formal skills of students have not declined precipitously. (406)

While I think there is every reason to agree with Connors and Lunsford's estimation of students' ability to write error-free prose, their notion of error ignores the powerful influence of the process of reading on teacher ability to see and respond to a particular feature of student writing. Instead of viewing their findings just as evidence that students make no more formal errors in language conventions in the late 1980s than they did in 1917 or 1930, we might also say that the evidence could mean that teachers still mark about the same percentage of errors as they always have—though data from Ball's (1997) work show us that there is a good bit of variation among individual readers. We might also speculate on just how much error a reader can mark and recognize and still be able to comment on other aspects of student writing and manage to read all of the student writing required for teaching first-year writing courses. To see response as reading changes what we can say about Connors' and Lunsford's (1993) findings or any other data about teacher response, since we cannot ignore the creative properties of the reading process and assume that readers merely respond to stable features within a text.

CONTEXT

We must include in any discussion of reading the context of specific classrooms, teachers and students. We know that reading is a selective process and that meaning is not a stable entity, but rather the individual reader negotiates a particular meaning that is based on prior experience not only as a reader but within her specific role as a reader in a particular context. As such, we cannot understand the ways a teacher might read and respond to her students unless we consider the influences that affect such reading and response. For example, Melanie Sperling (1994) conducted a study in a middle school classroom in which she collected the responses a single teacher gave various students in the class. She found that the teacher responded almost entirely about grammar and correctness to one ESL student who had voiced concern over his ability to write correct prose, even though his writing contained no more surface errors than other students in the classroom. The two students who received the most rhetorically-based responses from the teacher were the best student in the class and a student who needed "kid-glove" treatment. In this study, it was clear that the teacher was influenced by factors beyond the student texts, and that she read student writing in different ways depending upon her sense of the students' needs. This influence of extra-textual features of students and their behavior increases the variety of factors that can affect the way teachers read student writing. In summarizing Max Van Manen's work on pedagogical understanding as it relates to response, Phelps (2000) notes that "It is interactive with the text, the situation, and most of all the person" (103). It is important to remember that when we read and respond to a student text we are influenced by a wealth of factors, many of which are grounded in our interaction with the student herself.

In a simplified sense, our political leanings and ideological commitments make us less than ideal readers for papers on certain topics or those advocating particular positions. Lad Tobin (1991) makes a valid observation about the gender bias in typical first-year sports hero narratives many teachers receive. These biases fall under the constraints of the reading process itself, but they are not wholly insurmountable. Louise Phelps (1989) notes that teachers as readers can become aware of their limitations as they mature and grow in their ability to respond to student writing. In a more complicated sense, teachers need to realize that all of our experiences with students, classrooms, curricula and institutions have the ability to affect the way we read student writing.

It is impossible to appreciate all the factors that go into a teacher's response to a student's writing outside of an understanding of that teacher's relationship with that student. An understanding of specific responses is only possible when we consider the context in which a teacher reads and a student writes. When a teacher reads a piece of writing within a classroom context, she reads to make meaning in a manner that includes not only an interpretation but an appreciation of the text as text. Reading like a teacher, as in any other reading, involves making a series of choices. The choices a teacher makes in reading student writing and the meaning she composes from this reading is based upon, among other things, her knowledge of the assignment, of the student, of the student's past texts, past drafts, comments in class, process work, work in peer groups and other contents of a portfolio, if there is one. In fact, it is probably a fruitless exercise to try to recreate all the factors a teacher takes into consideration when making an evaluative decision about a student text. An individual reading of student writing is based in and constrained by the structure of the class and the philosophy, training and experience of the teacher. To ensure that teachers can respond in an effective and pedagogically sound fashion, we should focus teacher preparation on the act of reading student writing to make appropriate decisions about how best to teach a specific student in a specific context. This focus will also ensure that our need to assess does not drive our purpose in teaching and that we allow and encourage teachers to use the richness of the teaching moment as the context in which to read and respond to student writing.

Although I have so far couched my remarks in terms of how context influences teachers' reading of student writing, context probably plays a much richer role in the ways people make meaning of language. Michael Halliday (1978), whom I cite in the previous chapter, holds in his germinal work, *Language as Social Semiotic,* that context is the key factor in the human ability to use language to communicate. A classic example of the importance of context in communication comes from Brown and Yule's book *Discourse Analysis* (1983) in which they cite the common occurrence of a doorbell ringing and one person saying to another, "I'm in the bathroom." Clearly, much more is communicated between these two people than a person's location in the house because of the context of the doorbell and what it means to be in the bathroom in our society. This example illustrates the importance of context in people's ability to make sense of a specific linguistic message. It is logical to assume that teachers' reading of student writing works in much the same way. Without a certain context, it is impossible for a teacher to make sense of what a student has written. This context, unlike the two people who communicate a simple message about answering a doorbell, revolves around a complicated attempt on the part of a teacher to help a specific student learn the complex tasks involved in producing any piece of writing.

TEACHING RESPONSE

A good example of the importance of context in the reading of student writing occurred the night my first graduate seminar in assessing and responding to student writing met for the first time. After the usual routines of a first-day class, I had planned to have the students in the class read the same student paper in groups for different purposes. I felt that having them read for different purposes would illustrate the complexity of evaluating student writing. I was hoping to demonstrate how evaluating for different purposes allows teachers to make different decisions about writing quality. I divided the students, all but two of whom had experience teaching writing, into four groups of three readers each and wrote on a piece of paper the reason why they were reading the paper, so that only each individual group would know the purpose for the reading. I had one group read the essay as if it were a placement exam, and they were to decide whether the student should be placed in basic, regular or honors composition. The second group read the essay as an exit or competency test required for students to successfully complete a first-year composition course. The third group read the essay as if it were the first writing assignment completed by the student, and the fourth group read the piece as if it were the final assignment in the semester.

Three of the groups found the paper quite acceptable, either placing the writer into regular composition, exiting her from the course or giving a low B for the final assignment. The group charged with evaluating the first paper of the semester graded lower, with the scores ranging from D to F. I wasn't too surprised about the disparity in judgment from the four groups. In fact, I might have been a little surprised at how three of four groups pretty much agreed, since we had had no discussions about rating criteria, and they were reading for different evaluative purposes. What really did surprise me, though, was that every one of the groups embellished the situation. They created curricula, students and whole situations with which to guide their decisions. As I talked to the groups they assured me that they had to have more information in order to make the judgments I had asked. One student declared, with several of the class members nodding their heads in agreement, that she had to have a context or the reading wouldn't make any sense to her. The class was also interested in where the paper had come from, what I could tell them about the academic level of the student and under what circumstances the paper had been written. Some of the "real" background of the writer differed from what the groups had added to their readings, and there was some acknowledgment that the "real" facts would change their judgment about the paper.

At first, I left the classroom that night a little perplexed by what had happened. I thought I had probably screwed up by not giving these teachers enough information for a "real" reading of the student text. I had, however, shared with them the writing assignment and had, I thought, provided them with a context. It seemed to me that I had given them about what raters in large-scale assessment situations use. The more I thought about it, the more I realized that these teachers had not given a textual reading of the paper. In fact, they had resisted reading a text. They were reading the pedagogical context, the teaching moment; they were reading like teachers involved with trying to teach and make informed decisions about a student—which, of course, I had asked them to do, and which purpose drives teachers' responses generally.

This reading given by the teachers in my graduate seminar surprised me at the time, but there is reason to believe that their reading was typical of the way teachers normally evaluate student writing. For example, there is evidence from protocols and interviews that teachers rating placement essays make judgments about student writing based upon their knowledge of the curriculum and how well the writer of the text being rated will do in particular classes rather than upon the scoring rubric being used as part of the holistic rating procedures (Pula & Huot 1993; Smith 1993). This might mean that holistic scoring procedures work to place students in the proper courses not because of the procedures themselves but because of the tacit context the teachers have for reading the placement essays. In this way, it's important to note that context not only affects the ways in which we read our student writing but actually makes a cogent reading possible.

If, then, we are to emphasize the reading of student writing and the contexts that affect the meaning we can make of that writing, then what kinds of experience and education can we use to prepare teachers who would attempt to improve their response to students? Is reading and the many interactions with students that create and control the context from within which we can read a student's work too powerful a force to allow the teacher any kind of control? Certainly, the picture of student response that I paint precludes offering straightforward advice, like asking teachers to formulate responses based upon certain principles or having teachers respond at the end of a student's essay or write comments within certain constraints. It directs an emphasis away from having new or prospective teachers rank sample papers or comment upon and construct criteria for specific grades which are common practices in courses for teacher preparation (Qualley 2002). Seeing response as reading not only complicates the way we think about the commentary we can give students, but it also complicates the ways in which we can educate teachers about responding to their students. It has caused me in the last few years to change the ways I introduce and teach responding practices to prospective teachers.

Like most classes dedicated to introducing teachers to the teaching of writing, we read some of the scholarly literature on response. Although I often vary the activities around responding to student writing based upon whether I'm working with college or high school teachers and other factors relative to individual classes, there are at least a few things I seem to include each time. We always take class time to read some student writing, with the whole class reading the same paper. Without talking to each other I ask students to formulate one response, what one thing would they say to this student about her writing. As each student-teacher replies, I keep track of whether or not the response is positive, negative or neutral. I make no record of who said what, but I do share with students the totals for each category. As a class, we talk about the responses we've made and what we think they mean about the paper we read and about the act of responding to student writing. At this point, students are often a little chagrined, since we have been reading about positive and facilitative comments, and we all realize how easy it is to slip into more negative kinds of commentary when we're reading student writing that has, at times, many easy-to-recognize flaws. The next step, which we take either that day or in a subsequent class, is to have students read a paper in groups for various purposes, much like the activity I described earlier. The particular papers I use for the various activities can depend upon the ways I've seen my student-teachers interact with texts. Sometimes I use a text they have read earlier in the class. Once students have read in groups, they then tell the rest of the class what they thought and why they made the decisions they made.

The final step in the process is to include in a take-home final a student paper for their response. These are the instructions:

> Respond to the attached student paper. You should create the student and context for the paper and respond accordingly. You may respond on the student's paper, write her a letter, create a response sheet or use any other method that reflects your theory of responding. You should feel free to grade or leave the paper ungraded. Whatever you decide to do should be based upon the context you create and your theories of language and teaching.

Over the last several years, I have been amazed at the range of students that can be created for a single paper. The responses usually include some, if not extensive, reference to the context created by the responder. More importantly, these new teachers learn from such an activity that their comments must be connected to a specific individual in a particular context. These kinds of activities, it seems to me, foreground for teachers that responding involves reading student writing to teach student writers. As the activities illustrate, it is difficult not to fall back into certain patterns. Reading in groups highlights the many ways that individuals can respond and the constraints under which teachers have to work. The last activity gives the teacher a great deal of autonomy and responsibility, linking response to the act of reading and the educational contexts that can affect and control the way we read. Of course, I do not offer these activities as any sort of panacea, nor do I contend that these activities work best for all teachers. What they do, however, is demonstrate that teachers need to focus on the way they read student writing and to become more conscious of their procedures for reading and responding to student writing. As well, these activities exist within a framework in which teachers can learn to question the beliefs and assumptions that inform their readings of and responses to student work. It also strikes me that having readers create the student to which they are responding puts a new wrinkle on the methodology of having different readers respond to the same text (Straub and Lunsford 1995). When we highlight the generative aspects of teachers' process of reading, then we can see some of the reasons why they might respond differently, as they create and rely upon various contexts and pedagogical representations. We might want to refocus our question about what kinds of students teachers think they are responding to.

LEARNING TO RESPOND

Since it is possible that any and all interactions we have with certain classes and students might affect and control the way we read student writing, it makes sense that we look for methods to help us understand and recognize the influence contextual factors can have on our reading. Certainly, all teachers have experienced a certain dread or pleasure in approaching certain pieces of student writing. The next step might be to see if there are certain patterns in our emotions and expectations about student writing. If we were to notice that certain assignments seem more interesting or pleasurable to read, then it might be appropriate to consider the ways we are assigning writing. One way to respond to certain influences would be to read all student writing blindly, ensuring that we don't let contextual matters affect the way we read. On the other hand, a blind reading is a specific context in and of itself, and without knowing whose writing we're reading, we are in effect cutting ourselves off from important pedagogical clues that help us provide individual students with the most helpful responses possible. If, as I argue in chapter six, assessment is research, then certainly classroom assessment and response should also be seen as research. From the first moment we walk into a specific classroom and interact with students, we are collecting information about students, noticing the ways in which they learn, read and write, interact with us and each other. Just as the teacher in Sperling's (1994) study on response used her interactions with students to respond to them in different ways, so too do most of us consciously or not let the context of our work with students affect the way we read and respond to their writing.

Since we are in a sense continuously gathering and using information about students in our role as teachers and responders, it makes sense that we seek ways to make this data gathering more conscious and systematic. One way to do this might be to use a data collection template like that implemented in the learning record system (Barr and Syverson 1999). In their book *Assessing Literacy with the Learning Record: A Handbook for Teachers, Grades 6-12*, Mary Barr and Margaret Syverson include "reproducible data collection forms" that could be adapted to any classroom or curriculum. (See figure 1.) Such templates allow a teacher to keep track of all of her interactions with

Figure 1
Data Collection Form

Writing Samples

Please attach the writing with this sample sheet.

Dates			
Title/topic			
Context for this sample of student writing: • How the writing arose—assigned or self-chosen • Whether the student wrote alone or with others, in drafts or at once • Kind of writing (e.g., poem, journal, essay, story) • Complete piece of work or extract			
Student's response to the writing: • The context of the writing • Own ability to handle this particular kind of writing • Overall impressions • Success of Appeals to intended audience			
Teacher's response to rhetorical effectiveness of the writing			
Development of use of writing conventions			
What this selected sample shows about the student's development as a writer • how it fits into the range of the student's previous writing • experience/support needed to further development			

Published as a component of The Learning Record Assessment System™. For further information, call or write the Center for Language in Learning, at 10679 Woodside Ave, Suite 203, Santee CA 92071 (619) 443-6320. Used by permission.

individual students. While Barr and Syverson outline the use of these forms as the assessment system for a specific class, certainly they could be adapted by any teacher wanting to be more systematic about the ways in which she is thinking of her students' need for instruction and its effect on her response practices. Another way to be more systematic could be to create a grid-like template, not unlike those used by ethnographic researchers in classrooms, on which a teacher can quickly jot certain observations about individual students. Of course, more narrative approaches, like a teacher's log in which an instructor writes her impressions and observations about individuals, could also work here. The form of the data collection is less important than the creation of a workable system that helps teachers to keep track of interactions, observations and impressions about individual students. These data, then, can help the individual teacher become more conscious of the kinds of influences that affect and even create her readings of student work.

WRITING AS RESPONSE

Although I have emphasized the reading part of response, it's important to note that response also involves either the writing of commentary in some form or another or the verbal communication of some response. As I noted earlier, I mostly agree with principles advocated by Richard Straub (2000) who urges that we be conversational, that we not control the student text, that we limit the number of comments, that we focus on global rather than textual concerns, that we focus on the stage the writing is currently in and that we make use of praise. While I am somewhat concerned about the acontextual nature of such principles, I am more concerned about how we can couch advice for teachers in more theoretical terms, in terms that are grounded in some notion of the ways we think about language and communication. Just as we need to remember that we have to read student writing before we can respond to it, we also need to remember that any response we formulate needs to adhere to basic notions of how people communicate with each other. If students do not understand what we say to them, then all of our efforts at response are futile. And, unfortunately, there are many instances in the literature where students do not understand what their teachers are asking them to do as they revise. Melanie Sperling and Sarah Freedman's (1987) study "A Good Girl Writes Like a Good Girl" illustrates how a student and teacher continue to misunderstand each other. Mary Hayes and Don Daiker (1984) used protocol analysis to have students read and respond to their teachers' responses and found that students often missed entirely the message their teachers were trying to convey. William Thelin's (1994) study of response in a portfolio class found that students were often surprised and angry at responses their teacher had given. Jennie Nelson (1995) and Russel Durst (1999) have written about wholesale miscommunication between teachers and their students about assignments, response and other aspects of the class. These few studies are but the tip of the iceberg in research that documents miscommunication between teachers and students.

First and foremost, we must be concerned about communicating with our students. The same principles for communication that we attempt to teach our students should also guide our attempt to communicate to students in our responses. First, we must consider our audience, who is the student and where is she in the act of becoming a writer? It may be that for many students, being conversational, as Straub advocates does allow us to tailor commentary for a specific audience, but if we gauge our responses rhetorically, then we have a firm theoretical base for the types of comments we might write and those we might avoid. Certainly, traditional static abstractions like *vag* or *awk* seem inappropriate, since they might have more meaning for an audience of people who give comments rather than those who receive them. Instead, we need to explain as clearly as possible what we mean by *awk* or *vag* and, following Straub's advice, relate this explanation to other interactions

Figure 2
Moving toward a Theory of Response

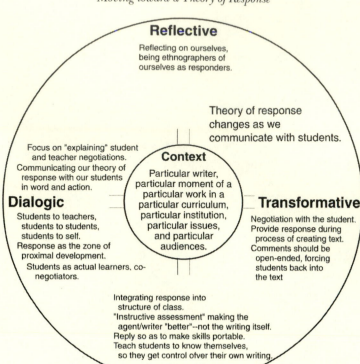

Reflective

Reflecting on ourselves,
being ethnographers of
ourselves as responders.

Theory of response
changes as we
communicate with students.

Focus on "explaining" student
and teacher negotiations.
Communicating our theory of
response with our students
in word and action.

Context

Particular writer,
particular moment of a
particular work in a
particular curriculum,
particular institution,
particular issues,
and particular
audiences.

Dialogic

Students to teachers,
students to students,
students to self.
Response as the zone of
proximal development.
Students as actual learners, co-
negotiators.

Transformative

Negotiation with the student.
Provide response during
process of creating text.
Comments should be
open-ended, forcing
students back into
the text

Integrating response into
structure of class.
"Instructive assessment" making the
agent/writer "better"--not the writing itself.
Reply so as to make skills portable.
Teach students to know themselves,
so they get control ofver their own writing.

Instructive

we have had with students or the class as a whole—not because these are good things to do, but because these kinds of comments situate our students as an audience in a communicative exchange. Consequently, advice about focusing on a couple of points and limiting our comments can also be reframed rhetorically, since providing a reader with a manageable amount of information that is linked to a main point is usually considered part of a coherent rhetorical approach to communicating with anyone. Overall, then, teachers need to think of their own understanding of rhetoric and use the same principles in their responses to students that they are attempting to teach.

CONCLUSION

My attempt to link response-to-student-writing with the princi-ples revealed in research on reading and writing is also an attempt to complicate our understanding of response and to move it beyond simple consideration of classroom technique. It's also important to note that, depending upon the instructional approach, response takes on a different role. For example, my writing courses mostly consist of activities students do on their own and in groups, so that my response to them is often the most direct teaching I do. However, in classes that structure time dif-ferently, response could be integrated in a variety of ways, since no matter what pedagogy is being used, instructors must read stu-dent writing and compose (in some form) a response.

During a seminar I conducted on assessing and responding to student writing, we spent three weeks reading and talking about the literature on classroom assessment and response. Once we had read most of the available literature, I asked the seminar to engage in a thought experiment in which we attempted to come up with a theory of response based upon what we had read and upon our own experiences as writing teachers.

I include this figure with the participants' permission and note that we called it "Moving Toward a Theory of Response." One problem we had in developing this model was that we wanted to include a myriad of factors that appeared to us to be happening instantaneously within the act of response. Because this model was composed after the class had read a substantial portion of the available literature on response, it reflects the concerns and wisdom of a considerable body of scholarly work. I decided to use this model as a way of organizing my conclu-sion, in order to get a sense of the ground covered in this essay and of how it compares to existing work on response. This will permit us to see what I have left out as well as allow us to see what contributions this discussion can make.

The model of response consists of a hub surrounded by four basic influences. This hub which appeared to us as central to the act of response is occupied by the specific context or occasion for response and includes but is not necessarily limited to the writer, the teacher, the class, the institution, the curriculum, the issues to be addressed, and the audience or audiences for the response. I remember how exhaustive we tried to be in creating a context that would control, limit and be constrained by other factors in our model. What's not included is any information about the teacher's process of reading and how various factors would affect the way she read student writing. This reflects the lack of attention given to reading in the literature on response. On the other hand, we did include a reflective element in which we suggest that teachers reflect upon their own processes of response as ethnographers. Certainly, my advice to teachers to monitor their own experiences with students through an ethnographic grid, the use of a journal, or some other template like that used in the learning record would fall into this category. However, to be fair, it seems that this reflective activity should be focused more directly on the teacher's process of reading, since reading is an interpretive act that constructs specific representations based upon several factors in and outside of the text itself. As well, there are no direct references to the act of composing a response or to the need to see this act as rhetorical—as being limited, constrained, and controlled by rhetorical notions of audience, purpose and the like. Clearly, any comprehensive model for response would need to be revised with a greater emphasis on the acts of reading student writing and communicating with student writers.

Further, there are several factors in this model that I have given scant attention to. One section of the model that is underrepresented in my discussion of student response above is the "dialogic," in which student input becomes a factor for teacher response. One reason I haven't addressed this more directly is that in chapter three I argue for a more central role for assessment in teaching writing, with students also having a larger role than traditionally defined. If we see response as communication, then we need to include students' input more fully into any understanding of what it means to respond effectively with them. Perhaps this notion of student response might best be understood within a rhetorical notion of audience, with students not only as the target of teacher response but as active participants in a "conversation' of response. As I argue earlier in this chapter, if we fail to communicate with students, then we have not been effective responders; we cannot be effective communicators if we ignore the input of those with whom we wish to communicate. It seems to me that response must be dialogic, since effective communication can never be one-sided. As this model notes, then, we must include our students' interests, opinions and attitudes in any kinds of response that we may assume to be effectively communicated. Integrating my treatment of response with this model could create a dialogic rhetoric of response that strives to enhance communication between teachers and students.

I think I have done a better job of including the instructive element of this model in my essay, though I think it's important that we not automatically assume (as I think I have done in the past) that teachers' responses are instructive. It is possible to use classroom practice to control student behavior or establish teacher authority, as in the research findings that depict response as focusing on the justification of teachers' grades. Another important addition to the discussion in this essay is the model's distinction between an emphasis on better writing and an emphasis on helping students become better writers. Certainly, this point distinguishes the kinds of responses teachers might give to students from the work many of us do as editors and reviewers, since in the latter instance our effort is focused on the text itself.

The transformative feature of the model is something that I have probably only hinted at. The model does not go far enough in talking about the transformative potential of responding to student writing. As the overall focus of this volume is to change the ways in which assessment is articulated and constructed, it is appropriate to emphasize the ability of response to change the ways in which we do our work as writing teachers. I second Miller's (1994) and Phelps's (2000) contention that those of us who teach writing need to focus more on the ways we solicit and respond to student writing; this is but one example of the need for a transformative notion of response. If we can change the ways in which we respond to our students in our classrooms and the ways in which we think and write about response in our scholarly literature, then we can harness the power of reading and writing to teach writing to our students, instilling in them the same wonder and struggle that guides all of us who work with language.

6

WRITING ASSESSMENT AS TECHNOLOGY AND RESEARCH

Several years ago, in an essay for a special issue in *Computers and Composition* on the electronic portfolio, I explored the ways in which technology had been applied to assessment, advocating that we use technology to link people together and to mediate responses to students rather than implement technology as a way to score student writing or respond to student writers. Writing that essay impressed upon me the ways in which technology had not only been applied to assessment, but how in many ways assessment had become a technology in and of itself. I later discovered that George Madhaus[1] (1993) had already been talking about assessment as technology and the problems this had brought with it:

> Changes over the last two centuries in the predominant ways of examining student achievement—from the oral mode, to the written essay, to the short-answer form, to the multiple choice format, to the machine-scorable answer sheet and finally to computer-adaptive—have all been geared toward increasing efficiency and making the assessment systems more manageable, standardized, easy to administer, objective, reliable, comparable and inexpensive. (82)

According to Madhaus, testing as we now know it is largely a creation of the twentieth century, in which social scientists eager to achieve scientific status for their work applied statistical explanations and technological apparatus to social and psychological phenomena like intelligence and aptitude. Along with the statistical machinery of psychometrics, testing was also pushed toward a technological approach since there was an ever-increasing pressure to develop means to test the largest number of people in the shortest amount of time for the least possible money. While this pressure for efficiency was also motivated by the prevalent theoretical orientation toward education and reality (Williamson 1994), it was also motivated in practical terms by situations like the need to classify army recruits for WW I—for which the first truly large-scale assessment, the Army Alpha Test, was developed. The ability of the Army Alpha exams to classify nearly two million recruits bolstered the confidence of educational testers who during the twenties devised the SAT exam and other measures that led to the development of multiple choice testing and eventually machine scoreable answer sheets. By the end of the Second World War, the testing machine was incorporated with the establishment of ETS in 1947.[2]

For writing assessment, the technological focus is perhaps a little less clear, given the kind of assessment that actually involves the reading of student writing, that has been the focus of this volume. The most obvious manifestation of technology in writing assessment has been the euphemistically dubbed "indirect" tests—multiple choice exams of grammar, usage and mechanics, which are unfortunately alive and well. For example, the COMPASS test currently marketed by American College Testing (ACT) for college placement contains no writing at all, measuring only how well students edit a passage on computer. It has been given to over 750,000 students during the last few years. ACT's claims for the validity of the COMPASS are based on the same criteria used for other indirect tests of writing (see the discussion of Camp's explanation in chapter two for more details), namely that editing is part of the domain of skills necessary for writing and that there is a strong enough correlation between COMPASS scores and scores on essay exams in studies undertaken by ACT. Historically, writing assessment's technological focus has been fueled by its continuing emphasis on the technical problem of providing high enough rates of interrater reliability.

Since at least 1912 (Starch and Elliott) the use of essays to measure student writing ability was considered suspect because of the lack of agreement on scores from independent readers. The College Entrance Examination Board continued the use of essay-type tests into the 1940s. In 1937, the Board introduced the Scholastic Achievement Tests (SAT) as an experiment for students wishing to compete for scholarships. This SAT could be administered in one day, and was scheduled in April. This allowed colleges and universities to receive information on applicants much earlier than the more traditional essay exams, which were scheduled in June, after school commencement and which took an entire week to administer. By the early 1940s, the April examinations had grown in popularity. The Board had lifted the scholarship restrictions in 1939, allowing any college-bound student to take the exam. The number of students taking the April exams grew, while the numbers for the June examinations shrank. In 1942, the Board announced a series of new policies for examinations that were designed to aid the rapid enrollment and matriculation of students during America's wartime. Among these policies was the complete abolition of essay testing (Fuess 1967). In response to a strong backlash against the scrapping of essay exams, the Board instituted a one-hour English Composition Test in 1943 as one of its achievement tests (Fuess 1967). Eventually, the use of indirect measures solved the interrater reliability problem, since these exams did not involve the reading and scoring of student writing. In the 1950s, interlinear exercises were developed in which students were to correct a text that contained specified errors (the format of the COMPASS). By the 1960s, a team of ETS researchers (Godshalk, Swineford and Coffman 1966) were able to devise methods that ensured enough agreement among researchers to make the scoring of essays statistically viable. Overall, methods for writing assessment have evolved from reading essays to make a specific decision, to multiple choice tests, to holistic, analytic and primary trait scoring, to computer scoring of student writing. As various technologies were developed throughout the twentieth century, they were applied to writing assessment. Now, it is possible for students wishing entry to graduate school in business to write exams on computer from all over the world, and for readers to receive training, score essays and relay their decisions by accessing a secure web site.

Clearly, there are some advantages technology can provide for the assessing of student writing. For example, writing placement has always presented real problems, since students have to write an essay which needs to be scored, so they can be placed into a specific class. Often the first time students are available to write is when they visit campus during orientation; this dictates that a tremendous number of student essays need to be read within a short time, so students can be registered for the appropriate class. Technology now permits students to compose on computer or even online, with readers accessing student writing from a secure web site, expediting the entire process—which greatly aids students and schools who need such decisions as soon as possible.

WRITING ASSESSMENT AS TECHNOLOGY

Understanding writing assessment as technology is important because it gives us a lens through which to consider the ways in which assessment procedures have evolved. Also, it's important to keep in mind that technologies can be imbued with various political and ideological orientations. Perhaps the most famous example of technology and ideology comes from Langdon Winner (1986) who points out that the underpasses on the Long Island Expressway were deliberately designed so that busses would not fit through them. The idea behind such a design was that it would keep people off the island who could not afford their own vehicles and relied on public transportation. As I mention in the next chapter, the Standford Binet IQ test was actually renormed in the 1930s after initial versions showed that girls outperformed boys. Technological projects like intelligence testing or engineering have the veneer of being objective, scientific and socially disinterested, but as studies in the rhetoric of science and these two examples demonstrate, all human activity is situated in specific ideas about society and social order, and all professional practices have theoretical, epistemological and material consequences. Technology, like any other human activity, can help to promote certain social, political and ideological values.

In his book, *Critical Theory of Technology*, Andrew Feenberg identifies two main attitudes toward technology: instrumental and substantive. The less common substantive attitude toward technology refers to people who believe that "technology constitutes a new type of social system that restructures the entire social world as an object of control" (1991, 7). Instrumental, the more common attitude toward technology, the one which sums up the way in which assessment and technology have been linked together, stipulates that "Technologies are 'tools' standing ready to serve the purposes of its users. Technology is deemed neutral without valuative content of its own" (1991, 5). In this way, technology can be used in many different ways merely as a tool to accomplish a particular task. Unfortunately, this instrumental view of technology as an ideology-free problem-solving tool can lead to an approach Seymour Papert (1987) called "technocratic" in which computers and other technologies are viewed outside of any specific context. The ability to accomplish a task or solve a problem is merely dependent upon our ability to devise an appropriate technological solution based upon the available technology. In other words, we do something because we can. Gail Hawisher (1989) adapted Papert's notion of the technocratic in coining the term *technocentrism* to describe the enthusiastic and uncritical employment of computer technologies to teach writing. Hawisher argues that in the rush to embrace computer technology for the teaching of writing, we abandoned what we knew about literacy, composing, and reading, focusing instead upon the kinds of instructional environments that computers made available, regardless of the ability of these environments to foster the qualities we know enhance the teaching of writing. In a technocentric approach, the ability of the tools themselves drive our practices.

For example, in his germinal chapter on holistic scoring in 1977, Charles Cooper introduces holistic scoring as a way of assessing student writing, no small feat considering that before the use of holistic scoring, using essays to assess student writing was considered unreliable, and multiple choice tests of grammar usage and mechanics were the only statistically acceptable form of writing assessment. Cooper goes on to expound the virtues of holistic scoring, noting that now we could now rank the writing abilities of every student in a school. Cooper provides no reason for why we would want to rank students in a particular school beyond the fact that it is now technically possible. Cooper's reasoning could be said to be technocentric, since it appears to be based on the fact that holistic scoring supplies school officials with the ability to rank students rather than on any other consideration of the ways writing is taught or learned or how this ranking could improve teaching or learning. What's important to remember is that while Cooper's idea to rank all students in a school based upon their scores from holistic scoring comes from a technocentric view of assessment, the results of such a decision could have widespread implications for teaching and learning of writing, depending upon who has access to the rankings and how they might be used to make educational decisions.

Cooper's inclination to use the newly developed technology of holistic scoring to evaluate and rank all the students in a school is representative of the ways in which writing assessment has been developed over the years. Because early studies of writing assessment showed that independent raters had trouble agreeing on what scores to give the same essays, writing assessment focused on how to achieve reliability, to the point of developing tests that were reliable even though they contained no student writing at all. Frank Bowles, president of the College Board called the writing sample portion of the entrance examination "an intellectually indefensible monstrosity" (Valentine 1980, 116). During the backlash the Board experienced after dismantling the essay exams, John Stalnaker, the Board's Associate Secretary writes in 1943:

> The type of test so highly valued by teachers of English, which requires the candidate to write a theme or essay, is not a worthwhile testing device. Whether or not the writing of essays as a means of teaching writing deserves the place it has in the secondary school curriculum may be equally questioned. Eventually, it is hoped, sufficient evidence may be accumulated to outlaw forever the "write-a-theme-on" . . . type of examination. (qtd in Fuess 1967, 158)

Stalnaker's blistering criticism of essay testing is less shocking than his complete indictment of teaching writing by having students write. For me, what's even more disturbing is that his words seem to have had great predictive value, given Arthur Applebee's findings in the late 1970s about the absence of writing in the secondary curriculum (1981).

In trying to account for why it took so long for the CEEB to move toward the indirect testing of writing through the use of multiple choice tests on grammar usage and mechanics, Orville Palmer of ETS writes,

> The Board regretted the authority of a large and conservative segment of the English teaching profession which sincerely believed that the writing of essays and other free response exercises constituted the only direct means of obtaining evidence as to a student's ability to write and understand his own language. (1960, 11)

Palmer's history of the "Sixty Years of English Testing" goes on to elaborate how "more complex testing techniques" were eventually developed.

The use of a multiple-choice test to assess student ability in writing certainly fits even a simple definition of technology as "something put together for a purpose, to satisfy a pressing and immediate need, or to solve a problem" (Madhaus 1993, 12-13). According to Madhaus, the notion of technology as a machine has evolved into a newer conception: "However, much of present technology is specialized arcane knowledge, hidden algorithms, and technical art; it is a complex of standardized means for attaining a predetermined end in social, economic, administrative and educational institutions" (12). In this way, it is possible to see reliability as a technical problem and the use of multiple choice exams of writing as a technology to solve this problem, involving the "arcane knowledge" of test item analysis, concurrent validity and psychometrics. In other words, a multiple choice test becomes a viable way of assessing writing because it is technologically possible, satisfying the technical need for reliability, though it may not contain any writing. Writing assessment has been predominantly constructed as a technical problem requiring a technological solution. Donald Schön's discussion of positivism and Technical Rationality, including his comment that "professional activity consists in instrumental problem solving made rigorous by the application of scientific theory and technique" (1983, 21), provides a good description and explanation of the ways in which writing assessment developed as a technology. For Schön, the importance of this problem-solving orientation is especially crucial in how knowledge gets made:

> In real-world practice, problems do not present themselves to the practitioner as givens. They must be constructed from the materials of problematic situations which are puzzling, troubling and uncertain . . . But with this emphasis on problem solving, we ignore problem setting . . . Problem setting is a process in which interactively, we *name* the things to which we will attend and *frame* the context in which we will attend to them. (1983, 40 [italics in original])

In other words, by setting up the technical problem of reliability as the main agenda for developing writing assessment, early writing assessment researchers ignored the way in which the problem was set and instead focused on how to create procedures for reading and scoring student writing in which teachers could agree. More recent writing assessment procedures (Durst Roemer and Schultz 1994; Haswell and Wyche-Smith 1994; Smith 1993; and others), which we have discussed throughout the rest of this volume, circumvent the focus on interrater reliability in various ways. Durst, Roemer and Shultz, for example, have teachers read in teams in which they discuss their decisions. Haswell and Wyche-Smith only use one reader for the initial reading.

Smith paired readers with similar teaching experiences and found that they agreed at a higher rate than those he trained with conventional holistic scoring methods. Had early writing assessment specialists followed Smith, they might not have discovered any reliability problem at all, since Smith's results indicate that when teachers make contextual decisions about which they are expert, they tend to agree at a higher level than explicit training for agreement can provide. One main difference between conventional writing assessment procedures and those I cite here is that holistic, analytic or primary-trait all render scores for writing; whereas, all of the newer forms render direct decisions about student writers based upon their writing. Technological approaches produce uniform, standardized and abstract results like scores, whereas newer approaches produce direct, concrete, contextual and applicable decisions.

The technological focus of writing assessment can be seen in the recent and continuing creation of computer programs that can "simulate" human readings by providing the same score a trained reader might give the same essay. The emphasis on reliability that first led to the development of indirect tests of writing and then holistic, primary-trait and analytic scoring is now leading the development of computer programs to generate reliable scores. In order for a writing assessment scoring session to be deemed acceptable, it must display an acceptable level of inter-rater reliability, represented as a numerical coefficient computed according to specific standard statistical formulae (Cherry and Meyer 1993). Test administrators and those who read essays for holistic, analytic or primary-trait scoring must follow specific procedures for training, reading, and scoring student papers[3] or portfolios. Within these scoring sessions that are geared to providing consistency in scoring, readers are often asked to suspend their own reading of student writing in order to read according to the guidelines specified in the rubric, so that raters can agree (Broad 1994; Bunch and Schneider 1993). Training readers is sometimes referred to as a calibration process, as if readers, like some machine, are calibrated to agree

(Bunch and Schneider 1993; Hake 1986). As White (1994) and others have detailed, holistic scoring[4] requires adherence to a fairly tight protocol of procedures.

The main result of this tightly scripted procedure for reading student writing is the production of reliable scores for writing assessment. Other results include the creation of a reading system that favors one particular interpretation of reading and student writing ability. There is no room for the diversity of opinion and interpretation that mark most reading (Broad 1994; Elbow and Yancey 1994; Williamson 1993). In a description of a training session, Robert Broad (1994) illustrates the ways in which interpretation and meaning are predetermined through the use of anchor papers and training rubrics, so that readers are compelled to read student writing from one specific point of view. More recently, Pamela Moss and Aaron Schutz (2001) illustrate the same phenomenon in describing the creation of standards for teacher certification. This way of reading is antithetical to the kinds of meaning making and interpretation that most often accompanies the way in which people come to value certain kinds of texts (Smith 1988). As Elbow and Yancey (1994) note, reading in a scoring session designed for agreement alters the focus present in much reading in English, since different, innovative and novel interpretations are valued in reading literature, whereas in reading student writing, such diversity is all but abolished. In fact, Edward Wolfe, in a series of research studies, has found that raters who agree most often with others in scoring sessions actually read in a more limited and focused manner that emulates the principles fostered in training and in the scoring rubric (Wolfe 1997; Wolfe, Kao, and Ranney 1998; Wolfe and Ranney 1996).

It is safe to say that holistic and other scoring methods that rely on rubrics and training and are designed specifically to foster agreement among raters produce an environment for reading that is unlike any in which most of us ever read. What's more crucial in understanding the machine-like orientation of holistic, analytic and primary-trait scoring is that little attention is directed toward anything else. For example, Englehard, Gordon, and Gabrielson (1992) conducted a study involving the holistic scoring of over one hundred thousand pieces of student writing and used this to make important points about gender and writing ability, even though the scoring rubric is predominantly focused on usage, grammar and mechanics. These kinds of scoring procedures are best understood as a technology designed to solve the problem of inconsistency in scoring. The result of this technological approach to writing assessment is that people choose to conduct holistic scoring sessions to produce numerical scores for students regardless of the decisions they wish to make. What's probably even more problematic is that attention during and after a holistic scoring session is focused on the technical aspects of scoring, like the construction of the scoring guideline or rubric, the selection of anchor papers, and, most importantly, the generation of reliable scores. Writing assessment practitioners are more like technicians than anything else as they attend to the machinery of the scoring session, since these are the important aspects that will make the assessments acceptable and valuable. Scoring sessions are standardized routines whose very acceptability depends upon the strict adherence to certain procedures that were designed to ensure the reliable production of scores for student essays.

The overwhelming technological focus of writing assessment has created a climate in which technical expertise is continually emphasized, and attempts to create assessments outside of a narrow technological focus are severely criticized: "Authorizing English departments to isolate themselves intellectually in order to engage in technically amateurish evaluation of their programs" (Scharton 1996, 61). In fact, English teachers who refuse to support traditional, technological approaches to writing assessment like the computer-generated assessment of student writing have been grossly caricatured: "A political stance that denies the importance of writing mechanics and resists all forms of technology and science is not good for writing instruction" (Breland 1996, 256). While Maurice Scharton's (1996) claim of isolation for English departments mirrors Pamela Moss's claim, which I discussed in chapter two, that college writing assessment remains isolated from the larger educational community, my point that the isolation Moss refers to goes both ways seems equally true for Scharton's (1996) claim. For example, he fails to cite several of the writing assessment programs developed in English departments—programs that I discuss throughout this volume. Not only do assessments like those developed by William L. Smith (1993), Richard Haswell and Susan Wyche-Smith (1994), Russel Durst, Marjorie Roemer and Lucille Schwartz (1994) among others defy the label "amateurish," they have, as I illustrate in chapter four, been able to break new ground, providing interesting and innovative approaches outside of current traditional writing assessment. Hunter Breland's (1996) description of English teacher's attitudes toward assessment, correctness and science has no basis in reality. Perhaps one positive way to understand these and other attacks by members of the assessment community is to see them as a desperate attempt to combat the eroding influence of their technological focus, clearly a signal that important contributions are currently being made by the college writing assessment community and others working outside a narrowly defined psychometric and technological focus.

WRITING ASSESSMENT AS RESEARCH

The biggest problem created by the way writing assessment has been developed and constructed as a technology primarily to solve the technical problem of interrater reliability is that it has obscured the essential purpose of assessment as research and inquiry, as a way of asking and answering questions about students' writing and the programs designed to teach students to write. The primary consideration in assessing student writing should be what we want to know about our students. For example, are they ready for a specific level of instruction, or have they completed a course of study that allows them to move on to new courses and challenges? When doing research, the primary considerations are the research questions. Once we decide what it is we want to know, then we can fashion methods to help us find out. With the current conception of writing assessment as a technological process, the methods themselves have become the most important consideration. Procedures like the construction of a scoring guide or rubric and the training of raters on that rubric have become more than just research methods. Rather than have the research questions drive the search for information, the methods themselves have become the focus of those who conduct writing assessments. The methods of writing assessment receive so much of our attention that they have, in effect, become reified as writing assessment itself.

Instead of devoting assessment to asking and answering questions about student writing or its teaching, those conducting assessment spend their time worrying about and perfecting the technical aspects of scoring student writing. Although we have, as Yancey (1999) notes, seen the evolution of writing assessment from multiple-choice exams to single essays to portfolios, most student writing is still assessed using holistic or other scoring methods that require rubrics, rater training and the like. In other words, we have changed the sample of student performance from answers on multiple-choice tests of usage and mechanics to multiple writing samples, but we are still using the same research methods supported by the same theoretical and epistemological orientation (see chapter four) to render decisions about students. This ongoing reliance on these specific methods for research continue to foster the technological values that led to their development in the first place. While the multiple texts in a portfolio provide an opportunity for recognizing various kinds of texts and student ability in writing those texts (Belanoff 1994; Berlin 1994), the technology of holistic scoring strives to render one true reading (Broad 1994, 1997, 2000; Elbow and Yancey 1994; Williamson 1994). If we were to change the focus of writing assessment from the use of specific methods to a process for inquiry, we would, in effect, be changing not only the ways in which writing assessment is conducted but the culture surrounding assessment, the role of assessors and the products of our assessments, providing the possibility for real change in the ways we think about writing assessment and the positive role assessment can play in the teaching of writing and the administration of writing programs.

As I note in chapters three, four and five, writing assessment is not something most teachers see as related to or beneficial to their goals in teaching students how to write. In fact, many teachers see assessment as a negative force because so many current assessment practices do not even attempt to address teaching and learning, yet they nonetheless narrow or guide instruction, since many high stakes decisions about students, teachers and programs are linked to student performance on assessment measures. Expanding the methodological options for writing assessment and for the roles of teachers and program administrators not only furnishes the opportunity for us to collect and analyze a wealth of new information about student writing, it also provides additional motivation for teachers to become involved in writing assessment. With writing teachers in charge of assessment, there is the possibility that the culture surrounding assessment can be revised. As I note in the next chapter, there appears to be no cumulative body of knowledge among writing teachers and administrators concerning writing assessment. What writing assessment culture does exist often revolves around a sense of crisis, in which assessment is cobbled together at the last minute in response to an outside call that somehow puts a program at risk. At best, writing assessment is seen as something that we better do before it's done to us. Of course, this sense of assessment is understandable given the current nature of most assessment practices and initiatives—in which writing teachers and administrators are expected to use particular methods that require some technical and statistical skills most English teaching professionals do not possess. Envisioning writing assessment as research, however, alters the relationship between teaching, learning and assessment, since the teachers themselves are involved in articulating questions

about their students, programs, and teaching, and are designing methods to answer the questions they have actually posed.
Questions about how well students are doing in specific classes
and on specific assignments also become venues for teachers to
talk about what they value in their teaching, their expectations
for their students and their overall sense of how successful they
and their colleagues have been in the teaching of writing.

If we see our task in writing assessment as research, it not only
changes the focus of the activity, it also changes the role of the
assessors. Instead of administering a pat set of procedures to
produce student scores and interrater reliability, it is necessary
to decide what a department or program wants to know about
their students' writing, their teaching and the overall effectiveness of their writing program. Acting as researchers changes the
role teachers and administrators might play because instead of
just being technicians who administer the technological apparatus of holistic or other methods of scoring, writing teachers and
program administrators become autonomous agents who articulate research questions and derive the methods to answer those
questions. A few years ago, there was a popular movement in
composition that advocated that teachers assume the role of
researcher in their own classrooms and department. This
teacher/researcher role can have new meaning for a brand of
assessment that brings teachers together to articulate questions
about how well students are writing and how well we are teaching them to write. This change in role accompanies a change in
power, as well. Teachers and their assessments can no longer be
judged on just how technically sophisticated they are (Camp
1996; Scharton 1996). I'm not saying that the technical aspects
of assessment research are unimportant. However, I do not
think they should be the primary concern. It is possible for
those in English to receive technical assistance from colleagues
in education, psychology, or measurement, creating the kinds of
coalition and connections for a field of writing assessment that I
advocate in chapter two. Instead of just focussing on its technical
aspects, writing assessments will need to be evaluated on how

well they articulate specific questions, provide data to answer those questions and ultimately analyze that data to effect important changes in teaching and program administration.

In addition to giving teachers new agency for assessment, seeing assessment as research can also further alter the often inherently unequal power relations in assessment. While few English departments can boast of any expertise in writing assessment, many English and writing departments do include people with experience and expertise in research. Knowledge about and experience in asking questions and deriving methods to answer those questions is expertise that English teaching professionals and others can use to conduct writing assessments on their own campuses. Not only does encouraging literacy researchers to become involved with assessment enhance the position and role of English teachers conducting their own assessment, it also creates the real possibility that we can become aware of new ways to gather and analyze data to make important decisions about students and the teaching of writing. Currently, most writing assessment is conducted using holistic scoring procedures developed by ETS in the 1950s and 1960s. While the rest of composition studies has seen an explosion in the exploration of qualitative research methods that reflect new concerns about the social, situated nature of literacy and the political and ideological issues of representation and power, writing assessment methods lag behind. Except for the locally-developed methods I discuss in chapter four, current writing assessment research methods focus on how to produce reliable scores among readers.

Employing qualitative methods that appear to be suited for gathering and analyzing information about literacy and its teaching should also alter the products that assessments can produce. New methods of assessment that employ qualitative methodologies can provide thick descriptions of the kinds of writing instruction and performances that occur in our classrooms and programs. It might be possible, for example, to categorize various kinds of writing instruction and student performances, giving detailed examples of student and teacher performance. Instead of just being able to say certain students can satisfy *x* number of outcomes or standards or other sorts of criteria that are easily assembled, quantified and aggregated, it might become possible for assessment to provide the site for rich, descriptive examples of student writing and development. In this way, we can draw upon the theory and practice in educational research that advocates a multimodal approach. Before this can happen, of course, it is necessary for us to begin to ask different kinds of questions in our assessments—questions that require us to collect different kinds of data and perform different sorts of analyses. Asking new questions, employing new methods, and using assessment as research are only a few of the ways in which assessment as research can transform what we now know as writing assessment.

It should be noted that current traditional writing assessments that are developed and practiced by reputable testing companies like ETS do involve much research. This research, however, is about the tests themselves—e.g., studying whether or not certain students respond to particular prompts in certain ways, or how student scores match up to grades or other indicators of achievement or aptitude. While it is commendable that companies research their tests, seeing writing assessment as research is fundamentally different; I am not talking about the research done on a specific test, but rather am advocating that the assessment itself be seen as research. So, while some conventional writing assessments can tout their research programs, they are still only providing a minimum amount of data on each specific student— usually the sum of two scores he or she receives. As current theories of validity advocate, writing assessment as research opens up the possibility that we collect various kinds of information about students before we can make important educational decisions. Test development research on technical matters is quite different from arguing that we must collect and analyze richer information to make important decisions about students.

Seeing writing assessment as research also gives us a powerful lens to view its development and history. For example, Yancey characterizes the history of writing assessment as series of waves:

> One way to historicize those changes is to think of them as occur-
> ring in overlapping waves, with one wave feeding into another but
> without completely displacing waves that came before. These trends
> marked by the waves are just that: trends that constitute a general
> forward movement, at least chronologically, but a movement that is
> composed of both kinds of waves, those that move forward and
> those that don't. (1999, 483)

According to Yancey, writing assessment history has not
moved forward in any orderly fashion, so she offers the
metaphor of successive waves. The wave metaphor allows her to
describe how some things like multiple samples of student writing, part of a new wave, have changed, whereas holistic scoring,
part of an older wave, has not changed. In this characterization
of writing assessment, we don't always know what a new wave
will bring or what will be left behind.

However, if we think about writing assessment as research, it
may be possible to predict what will change and what will
remain the same. For example, if we think of writing assessment
as research, then we can separate writing assessment into the
sample of what students produce and the way in which this sample is analyzed to make a decision. Yancey characterizes writing
assessment history waves according to the following scheme:

> During the first wave (1950–1970), writing assessment took the
> form of objective tests; during the second (1970–1986), it took the
> form of the holistically scored essay; and during the current wave,
> the third (1986–present), it has taken the form of portfolio assess-
> ment and of programmatic assessment. (1999, 484)

In each of Yancey's waves, what changes is the sample of what
students produce. For example, in the first wave, students provide information about their knowledge of usage, grammar and
mechanics. This information is collected in a multiple-choice
format, which is by definition reliable, and is used to make a
decision about student's ability to write. In the second wave, a
single sample of student writing is produced, and this sample is
read by readers trained to agree on a specific scoring guideline,

to produce reliable scores (the same aim of the multiple-choice tests). In the third wave, the sample changes again, since students submit multiple samples of their writing, but the analysis of this writing can remain the same, since the two portfolio programs at Michigan and Miami that Yancey refers to use holistic scoring to arrive at decisions about the portfolios. What's apparent from her discussion is that what changes in each of the waves Yancey describes is the sample of student work, while the unit of analysis can remain the same. Yancey's focus on just the sample of student work and her lack of interest in the way the work is analyzed is even more apparent in her statement about the scoring system developed by William L. Smith, which she calls a "second wave holistic model" (1999, 496). Yet Smith (1993) actually developed and compared his expert reading system in opposition to the holistic method he was currently working with. Since Smith used a single sample of student writing, Yancey calls it holistic, even though Smith's method of analyzing the sample was radically different from holistic scoring because it contained no rubrics, rater training or other procedures associated with holistic scoring. If viewed solely in terms of the sample of student writing, the importance of Smith's groundbreaking work (which I refer to throughout this volume) is lost. Clearly, seeing writing assessment as research can be a powerful and important lens through which to view its development.

It is also important in a discussion of writing assessment as research to note that it is not enough to merely raise questions about the amount and quality of information we collect about students and how well we analyze that information to make decisions about that student and others in our programs. We must also ask questions about the methods we are using to conduct this research on assessment. That is, we must not only turn our research gaze outward toward our students and programs but inward toward the methods we are using to research and evaluate our students and programs. This kind of research is often referred to as validation. As I argue in chapter two, validity is often presented in a much simplified form in the college assessment literature. Instead of just viewing validity as whether or not an assessment measures what it purports to measure (White 1994; Yancey 1999), it's important and necessary for us to consider the work of major validity theorists like Samuel Messick (1989a, 1989b) and Lee Cronbach (1988, 1989). Although I mention the importance of validity in chapter two and cite definitions offered by Messick (1989a) and Cronbach (1988) in chapter four, I would like to conclude this chapter by using the current conceptions of validity in an extended example to illustrate the important ways in which research can improve and transform writing assessment practice. In addition, it is crucial not only that we extend our understanding of assessment as research to include the data we collect and analyze to make decisions about students, but also that we take responsibility to research our own assessments.

THE VALIDATION PROCESS AS RESEARCH

One of the most interesting examples of writing assessment as research comes from the work of William L. Smith (1993), which I discuss in some detail in chapter four and in other places throughout this volume. Although Smith created the first placement system that did not rely on holistic scoring or other methods derived from measurement specialists and psychometric theories, he didn't start out to do this. In a discussion of writing assessment as research, what's important to note is that Smith's placement system was a result of several research studies he undertook to uncover what he perceived to be a forty percent error rate in placement. Smith's (1993) series of research studies permitted him to ascertain that his program did not in fact contain such a large rate of error. In addition, he was able to discover many other things about the way in which students were placed, how student essays were being read and how well students performed in the classes into which they were being placed. In a very real sense, what Smith did was to conduct validation research on his program with the ultimate end of revising completely the way in which his program placed students.

Smith's research illustrates that the process of validation research demands that we either supply information and analysis to support the decisions we're making about students or create new procedures that are supported by the data we collect and analyze.

I'm going to outline the kinds of validation research we conducted at the University of Louisville to justify the use of state-mandated portfolios to place students into first-year writing courses, but before I do that, I'd like to summarize our discussion of validity from chapter two and outline the specific course of validation I chose. Although Samuel Messick (1989, 1989a) and Lee Cronbach (1988, 1989) are the two most influential validity theorists of the last few decades, for our purposes here I would like to focus on Cronbach's ideas. For Cronbach, "Validation speaks to a diverse and potentially critical audience: therefore, the argument must link concepts, evidence, social and personal consequences and values" (1988, 4). Cronbach's notion of validity as argument seems to me particularly relevant for those who teach writing and are interested in its assessment, since it lends a rhetorical framework for establishing the validity of making decisions based upon specific writing assessments. While writing teachers and program administrators tend not to be knowledgeable about the technical aspects of measurement and validation, they are comfortable with and knowledgeable about the ways in which arguments can be crafted. Seeing validation as argument also illustrates some important features of validity.

For one, validity will always be partial, or as Messick notes, validity is "an evaluative judgment of the *degree* to which empirical evidence and theoretical rationales support the adequacy and appropriateness of inferences and actions based upon test scores or other modes of assessment" (1989b, 13 [italics mine]). An argument is always partial since it is possible that some will be persuaded and others not. According to Lorrie Shephard, "In the context of test evaluation, Cronbach reminds us that construct validation cannot produce definitive conclusions and cannot ever be finished (1993, 430). The partiality of argument and validity is based upon the truism that "What is persuasive depends upon the beliefs in a community" (Cronbach, 1989, 152). Richard Haswell and Susan McLeod (1997), in their chapter on writing-across-the-curriculum assessment, illustrate this by discussing the ways in which different academic and administrative audiences respond best to various types of reports and documents on program assessment. Argument and validation, then, necessitate that we consider audience. This notion of audience in argument is often seen as addressing the ideas of others, what others' arguments might be, and how we might persuade them anyway. In validity theory, a more formalized notion of this idea of audience consideration is called "rival hypothesis testing" which "requires exposing interpretations to counter explanations and designing studies in such a way that competing interpretations can be evaluated fairly" (Shephard 1993, 420). As well, we ask other audiences or constituencies for possible rival hypotheses in order to generate validation procedures that are as persuasive as possible. One last element of validation as argument is specificity. Just as arguments need to be specific in order to be persuasive, so too validation involves looking at a particular use of a specific measure:

> To call Test A valid or Test B invalid is illogical. Particular interpretations are what we validate. To say "the evidence to date is consistent with the interpretation" makes far better sense than saying, "the test has construct validity." Validation is a lengthy, even endless process. (Cronbach 1989, 151)

I am fairly certain that after reviewing some basic concepts about validity, our attempts to validate the use of state-mandated writing portfolios for placing first-year college students into courses will seem far from ideal. However, the process of validation is important in and of itself. Pamela Moss (1998) notes validation should be seen as a reflective practice through which assessment researchers can scrutinize their own efforts. It is in this spirit then, that I summarize the procedures that my colleagues and I (Hester, Huot, Neal and O'Neill 2000; Lowe

and Huot 1997) undertook over the course of eight years to validate the use of state-mandated portfolios for placing students
into first-year writing courses at the University of Louisville.

We began the portfolio placement project as a pilot, at the
request of the admissions director and a school of education faculty member who had contacted five schools in the Louisville
area to see whether or not the students would be interested in
using the senior portfolios they were required to submit as part
of an overall assessment of the state's schools. The first year we
read fifty portfolios. In subsequent years, we opened up the pilot
to more and more students, and for the last five years, any student in the State of Kentucky has had the option of submitting
her senior portfolio for placement purposes. In the last four
years, we have averaged around 250 students, more than ten percent of the incoming class. Having at least ten percent of the
incoming class participate in the project was important to us
because without a substantial number of students participating,
we felt very limited in terms of what we could claim for the
process itself. Since our goal was to establish portfolio placement
as the standard practice for placement, we would need to know
how well it worked with a quantity of students. On the other
hand, we were/are aware that our pilot was a self-selected sample,
and that students who participated in the pilot would not necessarily reflect the majority of students who enroll in our classes.

Our first question was whether or not we could use high
school portfolios written for a specific assessment program for
another purpose like placement. We resisted the Department of
Education's offer to have our readers "trained" on the state's
rubric which has shown that these portfolios can be read reliably.
Instead, we modeled our reading procedures on those developed
by William L. Smith (1993), in which readers are chosen for their
expertise in certain courses. Over the seven years we conducted
the pilot study, we have continued to revise Smith's procedures.
Unlike Smith, we allowed just one reader to make a placement
decision. Our other revisions mainly consisted of streamlining
the process. Eventually, we came to have all portfolios read first

by English 101 readers, since most students receive that placement. Then, we asked readers who are expert in the courses
above and below 101 to read. In this way, our procedures emulate
those developed by Richard Haswell and Susan Wyche-Smith
(1994), who demonstrated that most students can be placed by a
single reading into the most heavily enrolled course.

The first question we needed to answer if we were going to
use portfolios for placement was whether or not we could get
students into appropriate classes. We answered this question in
two ways. Initially, we kept records of how well students did in
the courses into which they were placed (Lowe and Huot 1997).
For the last four years, we have also asked instructors to tell us if
their students were accurately placed into their courses. We sur-
veyed teachers from all classes about all students, so instructors
had no idea which students were placed by portfolio.
Additionally, we asked students about their placement and the
use of their portfolio for placement purposes. (Hester, Huot,
Neal, and O'Neill 2000).

Because this was a pilot project, for the first five years students
who submitted portfolios for placement also went through the
existing process for placement. This allowed us to compare the
pilot use of portfolios with existing procedures, which consisted
of using students' ACT score as an indicator of whether or not
they need to write an impromptu essay. If students scored lower
than eighteen[5] on the verbal section of the ACT, they were
required to write an impromptu essay. We compared student
placement based on the two different procedures as well as comparing how well students from different placements did in their
first-year writing courses. Although we have found that portfolios tend to place students higher than the use of an impromptu
essay does, we have also found that students with a portfolio
placement achieve as well as those placed with existing placement procedures. We have further found that both instructors
and students are happy with portfolio placement.

Because we do not require that each portfolio be read by two
different readers, we cannot report interrater reliability data for

all portfolios. We did, however, compile interrater reliability data for all portfolios that were read twice, and found that the level of agreement was equal to or higher than (one year it was 100%) what is normally accepted. Because the reliability of an instrument is an important component of validity (Moss 1994a), we began checking for the reliability of placement decisions from one year to the next. Readers are either given a set of papers which had been read and placed the year before or, as we have begun to do in the last couple of years, a small percentage of portfolios are read twice even though the student can be placed on one reading. We have found over the last four years that the degree of consistency is more than acceptable.

Although students from the first five years of the portfolio placement project were required to complete both placement procedures, they were also allowed to chose which placement they wanted. We have documented the choices students made and the results of these choices in terms of the grades they received and the level of satisfaction they and their instructors expressed about their placement. So far, we have found that students always chose the higher placement and that for the most part they were successful in the courses they chose. Although our original intent was just to find out how well portfolios would work for placement, we hope to use this information in designing future placements in which students can have the opportunity to make choices about where courses most fit their needs. Currently, Directed Self Placement (DSP) is becoming a popular option for many schools who see the value of allowing students to make to make their own decisions about first-year college writing placement (Royer and Gilles 1998). Unlike Royer and Gilles's system, however, students at Louisville who made choices relative to placement did so after having received recommendations based on their own writing. This seems to answer criticisms about DSP that suggest students do not have enough information upon which to base their decisions and otherwise rely on gender or other stereotypes, and that DSP lacks enough empirical evidence for its claims (Schendel and O'Neill 1999).

Our validation data even includes information about the cost of reading portfolios. Messick (1989) makes the case that validity should include whether or not to undertake an assessment. Writing assessment that actually includes the reading of student writing is much more expensive than a multiple-choice exam, because of the additional costs of paying readers. In fact, the move away from essay exams in the 1930s by the College Board was partly predicated on the fact that the newer exams were less costly. As portfolio writing assessment became more and more popular in the 1990s, Edward White (1995) and I (1994) both questioned whether or not portfolios for placement were worth the additional cost. However, during the Louisville portfolio placement project, we have been able to increase the hourly rate we pay readers and still manage to hold the lid on costs, mostly because many of the changes we implemented streamline the reading process. Over the eight years we have read portfolios, we have never averaged more than five dollars per portfolio, and in the last couple of years we have reduced the cost to a little over three dollars.

Certainly our validation procedures for the portfolio placement pilot have not been as extensive nor have they rendered as dramatic results as those undertaken by William L. Smith (1993). However, the process allowed us to make a convincing argument that has resulted in the University of Louisville's decision to accept portfolios as a regular way for students to achieve placement in first-year writing classes. The process, as I hope I have demonstrated, not only allowed us to make a case for portfolio placement, but it also allowed us to learn more about the best way to conduct portfolio placement on our campus. And, like Smith, we also learned some surprising things along the way in terms of students choosing their own placement, a concept none of us had ever heard about before we undertook the pilot program and its validation. This last point underscores what is perhaps a crucial distinction between assessment as technology and assessment as research. Following prescribed methods designed to produce reliable scores for student writing is probably never going to provide the opportunities for making knowledge that engaging in inquiry-driven research can often give us.

CONCLUSION

In truth, assessment has always been just another kind of research designed to provide us with information about student performance or the performance of the programs we design to help students learn. As Moss (1994a) and Williamson (1994) have pointed out, the need to attain reliable assessment has pushed for more and more standardization, until assessment, as Madhaus (1993) notes, has become primarily a technology for the production of scores for student performance. Writing assessment, as we mostly now know it, is a product of the search to solve the technical problem of interrater reliability. If assessment is research, then methods like constructing rubrics, training raters and the like should be secondary to the questions for which the research is being undertaken in the first place (Johanek 2000). Unfortunately, as I detail in the earlier part of this chapter and as almost anyone who has worked with assessment knows, these methods have become what most practitioners consider writing assessment itself. The result is that instead of allowing us to think about what we want to know about students, most writing assessments require extensive attention to the writing of prompts and rubrics, the training of raters, and ultimately the production of reliable scores.

Seeing assessment as research, I believe, is a way of bringing a new understanding for assessment as something that all of us who work in education might and should want to take part in, whether it be for the ethical reasons Larry Beason (2000) argues for or for more programmatic, pedagogical or theoretical reasons. Writing teachers and program administrators can recognize the necessity of asking and answering questions about their students and programs, though they might rightly resist being part of a production line that manufactures student scores according to a well-defined but arbitrary technological routine. The role of teachers also changes dramatically when we see and implement assessment as research rather than technology. Instead of being technicians who implement a specific set of procedures, assessment as research gives teachers, administrators and other local participants the opportunity not only to control and design all aspects of the assessment, but also to build pertinent knowledge bases about their students, curriculum, teachers and programs.

In this way, the argument I make in chapter four about the need to move toward more local and site-based assessment becomes an argument about the necessity of seeing and treating writing assessment as research. It should be clear, given our discussion about technology and its influence on the development of writing assessment practices, why writing assessment ended up constructed as it is. However, once we recognize the ideological, theoretical and epistemological choices inherent in a technological approach toward writing assessment, we should also recognize that we have choices about how to construct our assessments. These choices are based upon an established literature and history of empirical research into human behavior and educational practices. In other words, writing assessment as research provides us with new opportunities to understand our students' work, our own teaching and the efficacy of our programs.

I also hope that understanding assessment as research provides an invitation for those of us who teach and administer writing programs to ask questions about the teaching of writing where we work and live and to use what we know about research into written communication to answer those questions. Discarding the technological harness that has historically controlled writing assessment can empower the people who teach and run programs to become responsible for their own assessments. This responsibility brings with it the need to know and understand acceptable research practices and to realize that theory on validity inquiry is necessary information for those of us who would conduct assessment research. For not only do we need to ask and answer questions about our students, teaching and programs, but we must also maintain that inquisitive eye on our own research practices, building arguments for the accuracy, effectiveness and the ethics of our own assessments.

7
WRITING ASSESSMENT PRACTICE

It might seem anticlimactic to conclude this book with a chapter on writing assessment practice, since the entire book has focused in some way or another on writing assessment practice, whether it be to emphasize its theoretical properties in chapter four, to talk about teaching assessment to student writers in chapter three, or to detail how to prepare new teachers to assess and respond to student writing in chapter five. By now, it should be clear I believe writing assessment theory is inextricably linked to its practice. Assessment is also linked to teaching, since it's impossible to teach writing or learn to write without constantly engaging in assessment. As I mention in chapter six, people often want ready-made assessment practices as if they were machines that could be purchased off the shelf; they'd rather not engage in a process of inquiry and research that requires the asking and answering of specific questions by members of a community of learners and researchers. Most of the time, I avoid providing examples of assessment practices, since I believe in their situated and contextual nature, and I think that administrators, faculty and students profit much from the process of developing their own assessments. Instead of offering examples of assessment practices, I try to give a working methodology that will help them to create their own assessments.

Throughout this volume, I've attempted to blur boundaries between theory and practice, noting from the beginning of chapter one that my aim is not to create a grand scheme or explanation, what I would call Theory with a capital T. Capital T theory usually means some sort of formal statement that details a set of principles. It is necessarily abstract because it is meant to cover many different contexts, situations and locales. It is deductive because the principles it constructs are meant to be applied to specific situations. Small t theory refers to the beliefs and assumptions within a specific context, situation or locale. Small t theory is inductive, since it comes from a specific practice and is not abstract or applicable beyond that instance. The two kinds of theories are related, and my distinction between the two types of theory is in some ways rhetorical, since I write about theory in terms of its relationship to practice for a specific purpose, resisting the common theory/practice split. As far as I am concerned, James Zebroski's definition of theory best fits my purposes:

> Theory is not the opposite of practice; theory is not even a supplement to practice. Theory is practice, a practice of a particular kind, and practice is always theoretical. The question then is not whether we have a theory of composition, that is, a view or better, a vision of ourselves and our activity, but whether we are going to become conscious of our theory. (1994, 15)

Zebroski's vision of theory in composition is applicable to many of the discussions within this book about writing assessment, since I have often worked to take tacit beliefs and assumptions about writing assessment practice and make them visible, hoping to make readers conscious of the theories driving their practices. In some ways, this book is about the relationship between theory and practice, with the underlying message that neither can be separated from the other without furnishing an impoverished version of either theory or practice. I focus on practice in this chapter not as a way separating it from theory but to show how its connection to theory creates a new understanding of writing assessment, in much the same way I've tried to create a new understanding for various aspects of writing assessment throughout the volume.

My decision to avoid promoting specific practices and to emphasize instead the theoretical aspects of all approaches to writing assessment has had some interesting repercussions. For example, in her article on the history of writing assessment, Kathleen Yancey (1999) differentiates me as a "theorist" from several people in the same sentence whom she calls "theorist-practitioners" (495). This distinction would be interesting and perhaps puzzling in and of itself, considering my long, practical association with writing assessment in several contexts—as a reader, scoring leader, designer, consultant and director. What makes Yancey's labeling of me as just a theorist even more interesting is that a few years ago in response to an essay I published, "Toward a New Theory of Writing Assessment," in *College Composition and Communication* (a revised version of which appears here as chapter four), Alan Purves questioned the theoretical basis of my work. His response was addressed to the editor of *CCC,* but Professor Purves had sent a copy to me, and in his own handwriting had written across the top of the letter, "Great article except for the 'T' word, Al." In the letter attached, Professor Purves (1996) commended me for my work and urged me to go even further. His only critique was my use of the word "theory," the T word:

> In general I am put off by articles that claim to establish or even move toward theories, since it means they are attempting to reach a depth of abstraction that is perilous. But in Huot's case, the attempt is praiseworthy because I do not see a theory, but a really practical approach to writing assessment.

I was thrilled that someone like Alan Purves had even read my work, let alone liked it, and I was anxious to answer him in the pages of *CCC.* Unfortunately, Professor Purves passed away less than a month later, and we never had our conversation. I have reread his response several times, and as I prepared to write this chapter on writing assessment practice I read it again. His comments are interesting within the context of Yancey's, since she sees me as a "theorist" (495), and Professor Purves sees my article on theory as practical.

This apparent contradiction is not only interesting as I muse on the different ways my work is received, but it also points to larger questions about theory and practice in writing assessment.

One of the problems that has permeated writing assessment is the notion that theory and practice are separate, and that because of practical considerations we haven't the time for theory right now (Gere 1980; Faigley, Cherry, Jolliffe, and Skinner 1985; Cherry and Witte 1998). In fact, as I detail in an essay with Michael Williamson (1998), I began my study of writing assessment after he and I had a discussion about the claim that holistic scoring was a practice without a theory. Of course, if we believe as Zebroski (1994) urges, that all of our practices are imbued with theoretical properties, then our goal is not to create a theory, so much as it is to understand the theory that is already driving our practices or to create new practices that are more consistent with the theories we hold or want to hold.

Although I continue to resist any separation between theory and practice, it is helpful to acknowledge that working from practice to theory or from theory to practice causes us to do different kinds of work, both of which are necessary and important. In extrapolating beliefs and assumptions from practices, it is necessary that we work backward from the practices themselves to the ideas behind them. In creating practices, we need to be conscious of the principles we hold as we move outward toward new practice. Louise Phelps's (1989) PTP Arc is an example of how new practices are created through a theoretical consideration of older practices, moving us towards newer and better practices. On the other hand, we should not ignore another kind of movement in Phelps's model, since according to her, we cannot move toward new and better practices unless we explore more substantively the theoretical implications of these practices. In Phelps's model, this movement toward theoretical sophistication is represented by going deeper as the Arc pushes us out further toward new practice. Working just on the practical or theoretical level requires only one kind of movement; whereas, being a theorist-practitioner or engaging in what is otherwise known as reflective practice (Schön 1983) requires a two-way movement that can also be called dialectic.

Whether we call it reflective practice, the PTP Arc, or a dialectic, what's important to remember is that without the dual theoretical and practical action, real change in writing assessment and its teaching will not occur. Without this deepening theoretical component, our practices cannot be substantively altered. For example, even though in the last thirty years we have been reading student writing as part of formal assessment, the theory behind holistic, analytic, primary trait and other procedures developed to produce consistent scores among raters is still based on the ideas that produce multiple-choice or computerized editing tests like COMPASS; we are reading to produce reliable scores. When William L. Smith (1993) constructed his placement system upon the expertise of his readers and not their ability to agree (even though they agreed at a higher rate than he could train them to agree), then psychometric theory that holds that reliability is a necessary but insufficient condition for validity, no longer supported writing assessment practice. Teachers were now reading the writing of students about whom they were most knowledgeable in order to make an appropriate, contextual judgment. In this way, current theories about the ways we read and theories of how literacy is taught and learned became possible beliefs and assumptions for a whole new kind of writing assessment practice. My purpose in this chapter, then, is to explore the idea of practice as a specific component of writing assessment. As I have in several places throughout the volume, I offer some examples of practice, though I hope to emphasize the theoretical and procedural activities that help us arrive at such practices.

Although my work focuses on the relationship between theory and practice in writing assessment, I think the creation of a more formal theory for writing assessment based upon the principles from validity theory could be valuable for writing assessment as a field of study. Working out such a theory would be an important way for us to learn how to talk about assessment and to understand the ways in which our practices are limited and can be improved. As I outline in chapter two, however, such a theory would need to recognize the important contributions of both college writing assessment and the educational measurement community. In fact, I think a theory for writing assessment would be a good way to link the different groups of people who work on writing assessment. As Pamela Moss has noted (1998), we also need to address the ways in which we talk about assessment and about how our discourse about assessment has created problems and limitations for the very students and programs assessment it is designed to help. Writing assessment theory could address these problems, linking together those who work in writing assessment and providing them with a coherent vocabulary for their joint venture. More importantly, a more formal notion of writing assessment theory would provide a constant reminder of the inextricable bond between theory and practice, ensuring that more and more assessment practices are held accountable to a theory that promotes teaching and learning.

THE NEED TO ASSESS

Edward White has warned the college composition community repeatedly that if we do not assess our students, teaching and programs, then it will be done for us from the outside (1994). Over the last several years, I have heard White's admonition played out in stories posted on the WPA listserv by writing program administrators (WPAs) in need of assistance with assessment. The story is always a little different in terms of the specific situation of the WPA, the program that is the object of the proposed assessment, and the person(s) or agency requiring the assessment. What remains constant in all of these stories is that a person who feels quite qualified and confident about her ability to run a writing program feels inadequate, beleaguered, and put out by the need to assess the program. The call for the assessment is always from the outside, from people who are not qualified to teach writing or administer a writing program. Often their notions of assessment are quite different from those of the WPA and others administering the writing program who are familiar with current teaching practices in writing. The usual culprits calling for assessment are deans, provosts, other administrators, or outside accreditation agencies. The responses from people on the list are remarkably similar, depending on the type of program being assessed and the individual situation. What's remarkable as well is that even though people who are experienced and qualified in assessment respond to the posting requiring help, there appears to be no cumulative culture about assessment practice, since similar requests are made over and over. In fact, one active list member well known for expertise on assessment has even referred people back to earlier strands on the list via the archives, since the territory had been so thoroughly covered earlier. These stories, although common enough on the WPA listserv are even more prevalent if we consider the number of times we hear similar tales from colleagues across the country. In fact, such stories of writing specialists who become involved with assessment are also a part of the assessment literature (Elbow and Belanoff 1986; Haswell and Wyche-Smith 1994). Examining some of the basic tenets of these stories can provide some insight into the many factors that can influence writing assessment practice.

A set of assumptions about assessing, teaching, and administering writing programs emerge from these stories to give us a sense of the current culture and climate within which much writing assessment practice takes place. First of all, expertise in assessment is not considered important for those who administer writing programs. Second, assessment is not even considered a necessary part of administering a writing program.[1] This separation of teaching and administration from assessment has created a stratified approach to the teaching and assessing of student writing that mirrors the split in writing assessment scholarship I discuss in chapter two or in the ways we use assessment in the classroom that I discuss in chapter three. The problem of the separation of the two has long been a focus of writing assessment scholars. (White's germinal text is titled *Teaching and Assessing Writing*.) Third, writing assessment is often a reaction to outside pressures. People like White have urged writing teachers and program administrators to become proactive rather than reactive, so that instead of being in a defensive position when it comes to assessment, we can take the offensive. In particular, White (1996) has urged writing teachers to become more sophisticated about statistical matters and the other technical specifics common to conventional writing assessment practices like holistic scoring. Fourth, people who have little or no knowledge about the teaching of writing or the administration of writing programs are often in positions of power to decide how writing and writing programs should be assessed. In all of these stories, any kind of assessment culture or link between assessment and teaching is missing, replaced by a sense of urgency and crisis.

I'm sure there are more assumptions that can be extrapolated from these stories, but these four seem daunting enough to give us an entry into talking about writing assessment practice. And, clearly the four assumptions are related to each other. Writing program administrators do not receive adequate education in writing assessment, because assessment is not commonly considered part of their jobs. Assessment and teaching, as I outline in chapter three, are considered separate and distinct from each other. Thus, the impetus for assessment necessarily comes from the outside; in a world where assessment and teaching are distinct, there would be no need to assess or to involve those responsible for instruction in assessment. Consequently, people with little expert knowledge about literacy and its teaching find themselves in the position of making decisions about assessment that ultimately shape curriculum and instruction.

The response from those in college writing assessment to these continuing scenarios has been to urge writing teachers and administrators to become more involved in assessment issues. While I agree with White's basic tenets about the need of those who teach writing to become more involved in its assessment, I disagree about the way it should be done. In addition to the need to work at the theoretical and epistemological levels I detail earlier in this chapter and in chapter four, I think it's important for those who teach writing to work toward altering the power relationships inherent in most calls for assessment. Because WPAs typically do not have even a rudimentary understanding of assessment and calls to assess originate outside of the program, WPAs often find themselves in a relationship where they have to be accountable to a higher authority for something they really don't understand. Accountability is often constructed as an integral component in assessment practice. In this way, assessment is seen as calling teachers and administrators to task, so that they can account for their programs and students to a higher authority defined by the assessment itself. Often however, calls for assessment and insistence on certain assessment practices are part of a larger political agenda to achieve and maintain power and control over educational programs (Huot and Williamson 1997). As Michael Williamson and I have argued (1997), however, it is possible to understand assessment as responsibility rather than accountability, as a necessary and vital part of administering an educational program (Beason 2000). Writing program administrators should be responsible for providing persuasive evidence that their teachers and curricula are providing students with ample opportunities to learn according to recognizable and articulated goals. Being responsible rather than accountable alters power relationships, so that the responsible person has control and ownership over the programs and practices for which she provides evidence. She decides how the evidence is generated and analyzed rather than being accountable to some higher authority who chooses the assessment regardless of the programs or people being assessed. I understand that my use of *responsible* over the more common term *accountable* won't change many of the outside and often unreasonable calls for assessment that those who administer writing programs receive. I do think, however, that if we were to become more interested in and responsible for assessment, we would ultimately have better control over the fate of our courses, teachers and programs. Rather than advocate a proactive stance toward assessment rather than a reactive one, I think it's important for us to recognize that assessment, like education and literacy itself, can have profound social implications. An often neglected but important fact is that assessment is a social action that can be used toward positive or negative ends.

A (RE)ARTICULATION FOR THE NEED TO ASSESS

Originally, assessment was designed to be a kind of social action, since it was supposed to disrupt existing social order and class systems. For example, the first formal programs for written examinations initiated in Ancient China (Hanson 1993), in nineteenth century America (Witte, Trachsel, and Walters 1986), and during the twentieth century through instruments like the SAT and organizations like the ETS (Lemann, 1999) were partly intended to interrupt the then current practice of awarding civil service appointments and educational opportunities based upon social position, family connections or other priorities unrelated to personal merit, achievement or ability. Unfortunately, as Michel Foucault details (1977), the concept of the examination is closely related to acts of punishment and hegemony toward those in society who hold positions of vulnerability. Tests and testing are constructed from specific social positions and therefore promote a particular social order designed to furnish the more powerful in society with a disproportionate number of resources and opportunities. Although there are many, here are two prime examples of testing as a negative, interested agent for social action. One example is Hernstein and Murray's book *The Bell Curve: Intelligence and Class Structure in American Life* (1994) in which African-Americans' lack of access to education and other important cultural institutions is defended based upon their lower test scores. The second example comes from earlier in the century (circa 1930) when Louis Terman, the primary developer of the Standford-Binet I.Q. tests, renormed the instrument after initial results showed that girls had outperformed boys (Darling-Hammond 1994). Tests as a pervasive, negative, shaping force on individuals by institutions should not be underestimated. F. Alan Hanson (1993), a cultural anthropologist details in his book, *Testing Testing: Social*

Consequences of the Examined Life, the myriad ways people are constrained, labeled and identified through a range of physical, psychological and educational tests. Unfortunately, there are many good reasons why tests and testing are regularly viewed as largely hegemonic exercises invested in reinscribing current power relations in American society, and why many writing teachers and writing program administrators would resist working in assessment at all.

This overall impression of assessment is exacerbated for those who teach writing, since one of the driving impulses in the formulation of new procedures for teaching writing that began in the 1970s was against current-traditional rhetorical practices that emphasized correctness and the assessment to enforce it. For example, because the COMPASS test used for college writing placement, which we discussed in the previous chapter, contains a passage of predetermined deviations from a prestige dialect a student must identify and correct, it defines writing and the teaching of writing in terms of the linguistic features that approximate the rhetorics and dialects of powerful groups. Regardless of the writing program into which students are placed, such a test sends a powerful message about the value of writing in the courses for which students are enrolled, when placement into the course is based upon her ability to proofread and edit a specific dialect.

Seeing writing assessment as social action helps us to recognize the power and potential for writing assessment to shape instruction, possibly enabling certain students while limiting others. It also helps to make clear that often assessments imposed from the outside have specific political agendas that are designed to profit certain groups of people. If we believe in the fundamental right and power of literacy for all students, promoting choice and social mobility for those who can complete a specific academic goal, then we need to design and implement assessments that will promote such objectives.

Recognizing assessment as social action requires a new understanding of our need to assess. Instead of assessment being a call from the outside for us to be accountable for our programs or for an opportunity to be proactive or assess before it's done to us, assessment becomes the way by which we ensure that writing instruction provides successful educational opportunities for all of our students. It allows us to recognize not only the importance and ramifications of teaching literacy, but it also alerts us to the crucial nature of what we value in our students' and programs' performance. How we value these performances are as important as what we value. An assessment is always a representation (Hanson 1993) and as such it has the ability to take on a life of its own. Assessments are powerful cultural markers, whose influence ranges far past the limited purposes for which they might originally be intended. The systems we create to assess ourselves and our students can have much power over the ways we do our jobs, the kinds of learning our students will attain and how we and others will come to judge us.

A NEW ARTICULATION FOR WRITING
ASSESSMENT PRACTICE

Ultimately, being able to understand writing assessment in new ways comes down to being able to change the way writing assessment is practiced. Since I believe that practice and theory are linked, real change in writing assessment means more than the number of samples we read or whether or not we write or edit on a computer. It is not easy to make any substantive changes in writing assessment practices because we must do more than just change practice, we must be able to disrupt the theoretical and epistemological foundations upon which the assessments are developed and implemented. Not only should we address practice on a theoretical or epistemological level, we must, as I outline in chapter six, also learn to look past the technological orientation of assessment and begin to see it as research that requires a community to ask and answer questions about value and judgment in order to make appropriate educational decisions. All of the chapters in this book advance a new articulation of writing assessment practice, whether it be the integral relationship of assessment in writing and teaching others to write in chapter three, reconceiving the field of writing assessment in chapter two, or the way we envision our ability to respond to student writing in chapter five.

In addition to the process of re-conceiving the various sites and features of assessment, we must also, as I've attempted to describe in this chapter, begin to articulate the role that writing teachers, writing program administrators and educational assessment experts see for themselves. As Larry Beason (2000) notes in a recent collection on the ethics of writing instruction, it is our ethical obligation to determine how well our teaching and programs are helping students learn to write. Preparation for a career in writing program administration should also include instruction in the rudiments of writing assessment, and administrators should count the assessment of their programs as an ongoing part of the job. In other words, instead of seeing ourselves as proactive rather than reactive in writing assessment— where we assess before being asked to—understanding writing assessment as a vital and important site for social action can support teachers and protect students from political agendas and other outside pressures that can strip the importance and vitality of effective instruction in literate communication. We need to understand that assessment can be an important means for ensuring the values and practices that promote meaningful literacy experiences and instruction for all students.

In chapter four, I looked at some emergent writing assessment programs that are based upon the theoretical and epistemological bases that drive much current practice in writing instruction. In figure two of that chapter, I note the beliefs and assumptions that drive these practices: that assessment should be site-based, locally controlled and based upon the explicit teaching goals of the program being assessed. In formulating principles upon which writing assessment practice might be based., I would like to add to these principles lessons we have learned from other parts of the volume. In chapter six, we differentiated between technological and research-based approaches to assessment. Technological approaches involve an application of a set of methods developed by others and used across sites and contexts. Research-based assessment, on the other hand, requires that the community of teachers, students and administrators come together to articulate a set of research questions about student performance, teaching, curriculum or whatever they are interested in knowing more about. In an attempt to answer these questions, research methods are employed in much the same way that we might approach doing research on any other issue or set of questions. In chapters two, four and six, we discussed the importance of understanding newer and more encompassing notions of validity. We've seen that validity pertains not just to whether a test measures what it purports to measure, but also that it scrutinizes the decisions that are based on a test—how they impact students, teachers and educational programs. In addition to seeing assessment as research, we are also responsible for validating these procedures—providing theoretical rationales and empirical evidence that make the argument that the decisions based upon our assessment have real educational value for our programs teachers and students. The latter set of principles should involve ideas developed earlier in this chapter, which suggest that writing teachers and administrators should see writing assessment as part of their responsibility and should initiate assessment efforts in the same way as they might revise curriculum, supervise instruction, or attend to other tasks important to effective educational programs. Following is a list of some guiding principles for writing assessment practice, as articulated in this chapter.

- Site-based
- Locally controlled
- Research-based
- Questions developed by whole community
- Writing teachers and administrators initiate and lead assessment
- Build validation arguments for all assessments
- Practicing writing assessment

The initial step in any writing assessment should involve the people interested in and affected by the assessment. I'm trying to avoid using the word *stakeholder*, even though it is a common term in educational measurement, because I don't accept the implication that different people with various motives all have a stake in an assessment, and that all of these stakes and the holders who represent them have an equal claim on the assessment in question. For example, how can we design a writing assessment that satisfies a politician's need for evidence that he is tough on education and supports strong standards, while at the same time tailoring the assessment to measure the strengths and weaknesses of individual students. In other words, if we really believe that assessment is a necessary part of making strong, appropriate decisions, then we must treat assessment the same way we would other educational decisions. This is not to say that we should exclude anyone from initial conversations designed to articulate the research questions that will drive the assessment. On the other hand, if decisions based on an assessment must promote teaching and learning, as current validity theory dictates, then we must be accountable to those people who are most expert about teaching and learning—students and teachers. In most specific instances, disagreements among constituents in an assessment will be limited to a couple of issues—for example, whether or not they can afford multiple sample assessments like portfolios. It is important to note that although I advocate favoring teacher and student concerns, the process of validating an assessment acts as a strong check on allowing them to "do whatever they want," since ultimately the people conducting the assessment have to make an argument that any decisions made on the basis of the assessment can be supported by theoretical rationale and empirical evidence.

Although my way of "practicing assessment" favors the local development of writing assessment measures that privilege teachers and students, I recommend that any serious writing assessment initiative involve the hiring of an outside expert who can mediate disagreements, help design the assessment, and in

general guide local participants through the process of articulating questions, designing procedures to answer the questions
and implementing a strong program to validate the assessment.
As well, a consultant can draft proposals for assessment that situate the local project within the larger theoretical frameworks
available in the assessment literature and help write any needed
final reports. Involving an outside consultant is an important
step in answering concerns of some that English teachers or
writing program administrators might lack the technical knowledge to design and implement valid writing assessment procedures (Scharton 1996; Camp 1996).

In addition to formulating questions, the assessment should
answer, it is also necessary in the initial stage to make decisions
about the scope of the assessment, what decisions will be made
on its behalf, who will be given the information obtained form
the assessment and how this information might be shaped and
disseminated. In leading several workshops on program assessment, I have developed an activity that I call "Design An
Assessment Worksheet" that contains several questions that are
important in the beginning stages of designing an assessment.
Several of the questions on this worksheet (see figure 1) are a
good place to begin. Questions one and two, which ask what it is
we want to know about an assessment and where we would go to
know about it, reflect the importance of assessment as research
and underscore the relationship between what we want to know
and how we will go about finding out. In other words, the methods we use depend upon the questions we have. Points 1 a), b),
and c) are also good targeting devices, since they allow us to
look at different groups of people, though I also think we might
expand our targets for information and include such things as
curriculum and instruction—perhaps even sub categories
under a), b) and c) that would permit us to ask questions about
students' abilities in certain areas or different kinds of teacher
or administrator activity. It's important to understand that figure one is a generic version, and that it can and should be tai-
lored to a specific set of needs.

Figure 1
Writing Assessment Worksheet

1. What do you want to know?
     a) about or from students
     b) about or from teachers
     c) about or from administrators
2. How will you go about getting this information?
3. Who is this information for?
4. What use will be made of this information?
5. What form will the information take? Will there be a report? Who will write it?
6. What verification or corroboration will ensure the accuracy and consistency of the information?
7. How will the information be collected and how will the way it is collected help to improve the program being assessed?
8. Who will be affected most by the assessment, and what say will they have in the decisions made on behalf of the assessment?
9. What are the major constraints in resources, time, institution, politics, etc?

Questions three though five remind us that writing assessment is inherently rhetorical, since what we are trying to do is to create a document that makes a specific point about writing and its learning to effect some kind of action. In deciding what questions to ask and what data to gather to answer the questions, we also need to think about whom the eventual audience for the assessment might be. Richard Haswell and Susan McLeod (1997) have an interesting book chapter in which they script a dialogue that details the different kinds of reports that specific audiences might be interested in reading. Haswell and McLeod also note that effective assessment programs require different roles played by administrators, faculty and researchers. Important in these questions, as well, is the notion that certain decisions eventually will be based on the assessment. This is often a crucial component for accreditation agencies. It's not enough merely to collect and analyze data, we must also have a plan for how this information will be used. An assessment should result in a written document, or perhaps, as Haswell and McLeod note, a series of documents. It's important, going into an assessment, to have plans about what documents will be prepared and who will prepare them. I have often written, reviewed, or helped to write documents for institutions for which I served as a consultant. When I authored these documents, they were reviewed by various local faculty and administrators, and then revised according to their feedback.

Questions six through eight refer to the ways in which the assessment itself will be reviewed and validated. The previous questions on the worksheet look outward to the questions we can articulate and the data we can gather and analyze to answer the questions. On the other hand, questions six though eight also look inward toward the process of assessment, asking how this information will be used, how we can be sure that the process will profit teaching and learning, and how we can ensure that those affected by the assessment will not be harmed. Simply, these questions point us toward how to craft an argument that an assessment can and should be used to make important educational decisions. These kinds of questions are the beginning of the validation process, and they affirm that validation is an important component of the process not only after an assessment has been conducted but in the planning stages as well.

Question number nine is an important consideration for many reasons. Local, site-based assessment needs the support of local administrators who control the purse strings of their institutions. As White (1995) warned us several years ago, assessment done on the cheap is often bad assessment. Quality assessment requires a serious investment of time and energy from those who design and implement it. And, as I advocate a larger role for English teachers and writing program administrators in assessing their programs, teaching, and students, it's also important for the institution to provide necessary support for faculty who lead assessment programs in terms of release time and extra pay. As well, it is necessary to compensate all those who work on an assessment project, whether they read student writing or are involved in other types of data generation, collection, or analysis. Before an institution can ask for assessment, they need to provide financial support, and any English teacher or writing program administrator who proposes an assessment plan should include a viable budget.

TWO MODELS FOR ASSESSMENT

I'm going to conclude this chapter by discussing two models for assessing student writing and writing programs that are supported by the principles we have developed over the seven chapters of the book. The first model is based on an ongoing assessment of the first-year writing program I currently direct. Because this model comes from a specific site and program, there will be problems with applying it unaltered to any other program, though it is possible to adapt it to most college writing programs. The second model comes from a presentation I heard a few years ago, and that has been reported in the scholarly literature (Cheville, Murphy, Price and Underwood 2000). This second model describes an assessment of the Iowa Writing Project that was conducted to satisfy a funding agency who wished to have an assessment of the project site before it would continue funding it. This model accomplished its goal of garnering continuing funding while at the same time providing very useful information for actually improving the work of the writing project itself.

The first model takes place in the University of Louisville Composition Program, which staffs around two hundred first-year writing courses (English 101 and English 102) per year. These courses are taught by part time instructors (PTLs), Graduate Teaching Assistants (GTAs), or full time professorial faculty. PTLs teach for a stipend by the course. GTAs, who can be enrolled in either an M.A. literature program or a Ph.D. program in rhetoric and composition, receive a yearly stipend plus tuition remission. Full-time tenure-track faculty are required to teach one first-year writing course per year. While the composition program goals stipulate the number of formal papers for each class and differentiate between a writing-process orientation for 101 and a research focus for 102, they do not dictate a specific curriculum or text. All non-faculty instructors are required to participate in a doctoral-level seminar on composition theory and practice that is designed to prepare them to teach in the program. There is great variety in the courses and approaches that individual instructors take, and we encourage this diversity. Instructors have used thematic approaches as varied as basketball and surrealism.

This background information about the freedom that instructors in the program have in developing their own curriculum is important, because one assessment procedure we use focuses on whether or not individual instructors actually meet program goals. Every semester, all course syllabi are read to make sure they conform to the general guidelines we expect from each course. In this way, we are providing a mechanism for ensuring that curriculum does focus on the teaching of writing. Instructors whose syllabi do not seem to meet the general guidelines have an opportunity to make the point that they are in compliance or to revise their syllabi. Another way we assess curriculum is that we require all non-faculty instructors to compile and maintain a teaching portfolio in which they keep current copies of their syllabi, assignments, and all other instructional materials. We also ask that instructors write a reflection after each semester about how they feel their courses went. These portfolios allow the Composition Program to know what's going on in various classrooms, while at the same time providing instructors with freedom in course design and curriculum. The teaching portfolios also come in handy when instructors are applying for jobs or for admission to graduate schools. This kind of information about what people are doing in their courses can be collected without a lot of programmatic effort or expense.

While keeping syllabi and teaching portfolios on file provides an ongoing record of the curriculum in the various courses, we also have all non-faculty instructors observed on a regular basis. We provide observation forms that include a section for pre- and post-observation consultation in case the observer and instructor wish to meet before and after observations. The form also includes spaces for observers to comment on what they've seen and what they think about what they've seen. Observers are also asked whether the observation was acceptable. If they deem a class unacceptable (this has only happened a handful of times in the six years we have been conducting the observations), the class is visited again by a member of the Composition Program staff. Observations help us to satisfy our accreditation agency's mandate that non-full-time faculty be observed on a regular basis. In addition, many full-time faculty find the experience enjoyable and informative, since all faculty teach some writing courses each year. Observations also help to de-privatize the classroom, making it a more public space. As well, observations provide information on teaching that can be used to satisfy mandates for program assessment, and this information is collected on a regular basis without great effort or expense. Like their teaching portfolios, some instructors put a lot of time into their observations, using the pre- and post-conferences as a way to reflect upon their teaching.

The last component of our program assessment focuses on student writing. Because evaluating student writing is something that requires some effort and expense, we do not assess student work every year.[2] In addition, because we are looking to evaluate the program and not individual students, it's not necessary that we assess every student's writing. We choose to look at about ten percent of the students' writing in each of the courses that constitute the two-course sequence required of most students. Because we are looking at a limited amount of student writing, we can choose to look at it in some depth. This depth consists of three separate tiers.

The first tier of evaluation is comprised of teachers who meet in three-teacher teams to read each other's students' writing. In addition to the portfolios or collections[3] of student writing, each team also considers five students' high school portfolios,[4] and the writing done for their first-year writing courses, since this gives us an opportunity to compare the kind of work students did in high school with what they are doing in college. Teachers read each other's students' writing and discuss their reading with each other. Although teachers record grades for all the student writing they read, only the grade by the student's own teacher will count for the student. Teachers also characterize the writing for each of the grades. For each of the three teacher teams, we receive a list of grades given by each instructor and the qualities of writing for each of the grade levels. In addition, we receive grades for each of the five portfolio sets of both college and high school writing and the grades accorded for those portfolios. We also ask the teams to provide us with a discussion of the similarities and differences they see between high school and college writing.

In the second tier, we assemble a campus-wide committee, representing all the schools and colleges of the university, and we ask them to read the fifteen sets of high school and college writing, giving grades for each of the college collections and characterizing the qualities of writing for each grade. In addition, we ask them to discuss the similarities and differences they see between high school and college writing. The committee conducts its business via a listserv in which individuals can single out particular portfolios and papers for discussion. All discussions are archived to be part of the possible information to be used in analyzing the status of the program.

In the third tier, we assemble writing assessment and program professionals across on the country on a listserv. We send all participants the fifteen sets of high school and college writing, and ask them to give grades to the college writing, indicating the rationale they use for grading. In addition, we also ask them to compare high school and college writing. We ask participants to single out any individual papers or sections of papers for discussion. In using faculty from across the country to talk about student writing over the internet, we are following the pioneering work of Michael Allen (1995) and others as they have used electronic communication to conduct program assessment (Allen, Frick, Sommers and Yancey 1997).

The three-tier evaluation of student writing provides us with a wealth of information about the ways in which our students' writing is read. It allows us to conduct an assessment that includes the voices of people who teach in our program, people who teach our students after their first-year of writing instruction, and people from beyond our campus who can give us a sense of how our students would be perceived by those who teach writing, administer writing programs, and evaluate both writing and programs from across the country. Comparing grades and the characteristics for grades for each of the different groups provides us with important information about standards and outcomes. However, instead of imposing either outcomes or standards from the outside, ours come from the writing of our own students.

All of the information generated by the three tiers is reviewed by the Composition Director, the Assistant Director of Composition (an advanced doctoral student) and an outside consultant chosen from the third tier readers. These three people compile a report that is shared with all three tier participants before being revised. Generating such a wealth of information about student writing that is read by such a diverse group of people provides an opportunity for real discovery about the kinds of writing students are doing in the program and how successful different groups of readers consider this writing to be. Comparing high school and college writing should provide some useful information about the writing experiences students have as college students and how this experience builds on what they have done before college. This comparative information should be useful for both high school and college teachers, as it allows them to get a better sense of who their students are and what is expected of them. As well, the final report on the status of student writing should be used to revise appropriately course goals, faculty development opportunities, grading procedures, and other program guidelines and policies that the assessment shows needs revising or improving.

The second model was developed to assess the Iowa Writing Project (IWP), which had received a grant that stipulated that the success of the project should be independently reviewed. Although project administrators wanted to comply with the need to assess, they were also concerned with providing an assessment that helped teaching and learning—the overall goal of the IWP. "Project planners believed the best structure for the review was one in which assessors could act as colleagues, offering participants feedback about a small sample of their work and the work of their students" (Cheville, Murphy, Price, and Underwood 2000, 149).

Teachers were invited to submit portfolios of their teaching and of their own students' work. The IWP hired an outside consultant team to help design the assessment, read all the portfolios and provide feedback for both the teachers in the project and the outside funding agency. The assessment team read all portfolios, providing for teachers a description of the teaching practices available in their portfolios and a description of the writing of their students. They also compiled an inventory of effective practices available from their reading of teacher and student work. All teachers in the IWP received a detailed description of their portfolio and the portfolios of their students along with an inventory of teaching practices from across the project. The result was that teachers got an opportunity to look with new eyes at the assignments, curriculum, and instruction and at the output of their students based upon this curriculum and instruction. In addition, teachers were able to see what other teachers were doing and to make for themselves a comparison if they so wished. In this way, teachers received useful feedback about their instructional practices and their students' work, while at the same time the funding agency received a detailed description of the kinds of teaching and learning that were ongoing at the IWP.

This program assessment model does a good job of providing feedback for teachers about their work with students. While the model stops short of giving explicit evaluative commentary of teachers, it does give them enough descriptive information about their own work and the valued practices of others to allow teachers to take the next step, if they so wish, in looking for new and better ways to teach students writing. Although this model does involve the use of outside evaluators, the effective teaching practices themselves come from the teachers in the program and are not imported by outsiders. There is also a strong attempt to provide teachers with the opportunity to improve their own practices by allowing them a reflective pause through which they can see their work and the work of their students in the eyes of others without any explicit pressure or judgment. This model would work well for something like a writing-across-the-curriculum-program where content-area teachers could provide teaching portfolios and samples of student work that could be described for them, since the model provides such strong feedback for teachers. It might also be a good alternative for model number one described above, so that instead of looking exclusively at student writing, teachers could receive detailed feedback about their instructional practices.

Both of these models honor the principles for writing assessment that are the ultimate focus of this book. While both of these schemes involve outside participants, the participants themselves do not set the focus for the assessment or decide standards or outcomes for the programs being assessed. On the other hand, involving people from outside of a writing program or a specific institution in local assessment programs answers mandates for local assessments to be sensitive to standards beyond a specific locale or institution. In this way, the assessment is controlled by those who teach and administer the programs being assessed and maintains the site itself as the focus of the assessment, while at the same time answering outside calls for standards and accountability. Both of these models also offer legitimate inquiry into the programs where important questions are asked and answered, and the answers to these questions can be used to improve the program.

CONCLUSION

Clearly, this entire volume has been about writing assessment practice, since essentially I am interested in helping others create assessments that can advance informed decisions about the teaching of writing. For example, in chapter two I map the field of writing assessment, arguing for a unified field of scholars who recognize and respect each other's work and positions, while always maintaining that the main thrust of decisions based on assessment must be for the promotion of teaching and learning. Chapter three defines keywords in classroom writing assessment, differentiating between assessment, grading and testing, so that we begin to understand and teach our students the importance of assessment in writing well. Chapter four unpacks the theoretical assumptions that inform many assessment practices, arguing (as I have argued in this chapter) that to substantively change assessment practices we must move to change the beliefs and assumptions that guide the practices. Chapter five considers the connections between the way we read student writing and the way we respond to student writers, attempting to provide the same kind of "practical" theory Alan Purves contended I had advanced for assessment outside the classroom. Chapter six characterizes the ways in which writing assessment can be both technology and research, emphasizing the benefits of using opportunities for assessment as chances to ask and answer questions about our students, teaching and programs. In some ways, this final chapter has been about all of those subjects, as we have focused specifically on practice and have realized that it is impossible to talk about writing assessment practice without recognizing a myriad of issues, some of which were the focus of the "theoretical" chapters in this volume.

One of my favorite quotes comes from the scene in *The Wizard of Oz* in which the Wicked Witch rubs her hands together with a pensive look on her face cackling, "These things must be done delicately, or you'll hurt the spell." Although the Wicked Witch's words can be applied to many things, they are especially relevant to a discussion of writing assessment practice. The "spell," of course, is teaching and learning, and unless we apply assessment in specific ways, it can be irreparably harmed. (This potential harm of assessment for teaching and learning is a topic that I have deliberately tried to avoid in this volume, although it informs my treatment of the subject, especially in chapter three, when I labor against certain connotations inherent in conflating assessment with testing and grading.) In this volume, I attempt to downplay the negative side of writing assessment because in order to (re)articulate assessment as something controlled by teachers to promote teaching and learning, teachers must learn not to avoid it or to leave it in the hands of professional testers or administrators.

Just as I have argued in this chapter that we cannot consider assessment practice outside of our considerations of theory or our jobs as writing teachers or program administrators, ultimately to own assessment, we must learn to see it as a necessary part of understanding how to write and how to teach writing. In some ways, then, this book is about deprogramming a certain understanding of assessment—or perhaps "decodifying" it would be more accurate. I hope we can come to understand the necessary and important role assessment plays on all levels of learning to write and of documenting that learning for students, teachers, administrators, parents and public stakeholders. This type of conclusion, I'm afraid, leaves as many questions as it supplies answers—the main question being *is what I'm proposing possible?* Although what I call for is ambitious and far-reaching, it is possible. The kinds of changes I envision and advocate will not come easily. Unlike what Dorothy finds, the answers have not been with us all along. In this volume, I offer no definitive answers. In fact, I am certain that the practices I do advocate can and will be revised in a continuing process of validation and reflection. This volume then is just a beginning, a challenge for all of us who are dissatisfied with past and current writing assessment to create a new future.

NOTES

NOTES TO CHAPTER TWO

1. It's important to note that this proliferation was by far incomplete. A survey of placement practices in the early 1990s (Huot 1994a) shows that half of the eleven hundred or so respondents still used some form of indirect writing assessment to place students in first-year writing courses.

2. A good model of this working together can be seen in Moss's (1998) response to Haswell's (1998) validation scheme which has been central to this discussion.

NOTES TO CHAPTER FOUR

1. It is important to note that only a certain, "trend" sample of NAEP's writing assessment claims to measure writing ability from year to year.

2. Leo Ruth and Sandra Murphy have since reversed their opinion about the viability of field testing prompts, since they now contend that local situations prevent the use of prompts across student populations and educational contexts (Murphy and Ruth 1993).

3. I am pleased to note that in more than five years since an earlier version of this essay was published, many institutions, too numerous to mention, have continued to develop their own writing assessments.

4. Since the early 1990s, I have experimented with Smith's concepts in creating a portfolio placement program at the University of Louisville, which I described more fully in chapter six.

5. An exploration of this placement system and other locally generated writing assessments at Washington State University is the subject of a new book, *Beyond Outcomes: Assessment and Instruction Within a University Writing Program.*

6. While I arrive at this idea theoretically, Alan Purves (1992), in "Reflections on Research and Assessment in Written Composition," details the breakdown of writing quality as a concept in a study undertaken by the International Association of Educational Achievement on student writing in fourteen countries.

7. This movement away from psychometric procedures has been underway for some time (Barritt, Stock, and Clark 1986; Carini 2001; Faigley, Cherry, Jolliffe, and Skinner 1985; and others). There are many institutions employing similar, locally-developed procedures. SUNY Stony Brook, for example, has students write placement essays as part of a two-hour class on writing. The essays are read and judged by two teachers, one of which taught that group of students (Robertson 1994). At the University of Louisville, teachers have met in groups to discuss and evaluate student portfolios as part of an evaluation of general education. We have adapted Smith's scheme to read high school portfolios for placement, and the English Department piloted a program last year in which teachers' portfolios were read collaboratively as part of an institutional evaluation of individual departments.

8. Since Allen's first article, he has collaborated with his colleagues from across the country, Jane Frick, Jeff Sommers, and Kathleen Yancey to conduct a program assessment online.

NOTES TO CHAPTER SIX

1. As I explore in chapter two, unfortunately the educational measurement literature from scholars like George Madhaus is not commonly used by scholars like me from the college writing assessment community.

2. Nicholas Lemann details in his book, *The Big Test: The Secret History of the American Meritocracy,* that Carl Brigham who

invented the SAT had become so disenchanted with it and any efforts to promote it, that Henry Chauncey had to wait until Brigham died before he could found ETS (1999, 268). Brigham had resisted the establishment of ETS because he was aware of "the dangers of having a single all-powerful organization in charge of both research on the proper use of tests and the commercial promotion of existing tests" (79).

3.   Although I am focusing explicitly on procedures within a scoring session, it is also important to pay attention to the prompt, since variations in scores from year to year or session to session can often be attributed to differences in the prompts to which students write. (Hoetker 1982; Ruth and Murphy 1988).

4.   While White refers to holistic scoring specifically, these procedures are also applicable to the lesser-used analytic and primary trait scoring as well.

NOTES TO CHAPTER SEVEN

1.   This fact was recently brought home to me with the publication of *The Allyn and Bacon Sourcebook for Writing Program Administrators* (Ward and Carpenter 2002) that contained twenty-three separate chapters, only one of which focused on writing assessment.

2.   I originally designed this procedure to assess student writing during the fifth year of my tenure as Composition Director, since there was much work to be done before we would be ready to assess what we were doing. Unfortunately, the university was unable to fund the assessment for that year. In 2002, we revised placement. We are hoping to assess student writing next year. Although we have yet to use the method I describe, I include it here since it is the third component of our planned assessment for the composition program.

3.   We do not require teachers to use portfolios.

4.   All public school seniors in the state of Kentucky compile portfolios and may use these portfolios for placement into first-year writing courses at the University of Louisville.

REFERENCES

Allen, Michael. 1995. Valuing Differences: Portnet's First Year. *Assessing Writing* 2: 67–90.

Allen, Michael, Jane Frick, Jeff Sommers, and Kathleen Yancey. 1997. Outside Review of Writing Portfolios: An On-Line Evaluation. *WPA Writing Program Administration* 20: 66–90.

Allison, Libby, Lizbeth Bryant, and Maureen Hourigan. 1997. *Grading In the Post-Process Classroom: From Theory to Practice.* Portsmouth, NH: Boynton/Cook.

Anson, Chris M. 1989. *Writing and Response: Theory, Practice and Research.* Urbana: NCTE.

Applebee, Arthur N. 1981. *Writing in the Secondary School: English and the Content Areas.* Urbana: NCTE.

Armstrong, Cheryl S. 1991. Writing Without Testing. *Portfolios: Process and Product,* ed. P. Belanoff and M. Dickson. Portsmouth, NH: Boynton/Cook.

Auchter, Joan Chikos. 1993. Six Years of Decentralized Holistic Scoring: What Have We Learned? Presented at the annual meeting of the American Educational Research Association. Atlanta, GA.

Baker, Nancy Westrich. 1993. The Effect of Portfolio-Based Instruction on Composition Students' Final Examination Scores, Course Grades, and Attitudes Toward Writing. *Research in the Teaching of English* 27: 155–74.

Bakhtin, Mikhail M. 1981. *Dialogic Imagination: Four Essays by M. M. Bakhtin,* ed. M. Holquist. Trans. C. Emerson and M. Holquist. Austin: University of Texas Press.

Ball, Arnetha. 1997. Expanding the Dialogue on Culture as a Critical Component When Assessing Writing. *Assessing Writing* 4: 169–202.

Barr, Mary A. and Margaret A. Syverson. 1997. *Assessing Literacy With The Learning Record.* Portsmouth, NH: Heinemann.

Barritt, Loren, Patricia L. Stock and Francelia Clark. 1986. Researching Practice: Evaluating Assessment Essays. *College Composition and Communication* 38: 315–27.

Beach, Richard. 1976. Self-Evaluation Strategies of Extensive Revisers. *College Composition and Communication* 27: 160–64.

Beach, Richard, and Stephen Eaton. 1984. Factors Influencing Self-Assessing and Advising by College Freshmen. *New Directions in Composition Research,* ed. R. Beach and L. Bridwell. New York: Guilford.

de Beaugrande, Robert, and Wolfgang Dressler. 1981. *Introduction to Text Linguistics.* New York: Longman.

Beason, Larry. 2000. Composition as Service: Implications of Utilitarian, Duties and Care Ethics. *The Ethics of Writing Assessment Instruction: Issues in Theory and Practice,* ed. M. A. Pemberton. Stamford, CT: Ablex.

Beaven, Mary H. 1977. Individualized Goal Setting, Self Evaluation and Peer Evaluation. *Evaluating Writing: Describing, Measuring, Judging,* ed. C. R. Cooper and L. Odell. Urbana: NCTE.

Belanoff, Pat. 1991. The Myths of Assessment. *Journal of Basic Writing* 10: 54–66.

———. 1994. Portfolios and Literacy: Why. *New Directions in Portfolio Assessment,* ed. L. Black, D. A. Daiker, J. Sommers and G. Stygall. Portsmouth, NH: Boynton/Cook.

Belanoff, Pat and Marcia Dickson, ed. 1991. *Portfolios: Process and Product.* Portsmouth, NH: Boynton/Cook.

Berlak, Harold. 1992. Toward the Development of a New Science of Educational Testing and Assessment. *Toward a New Science of Educational Testing and Assessment,* ed. H. Berlak et al. Albany: SUNY Press.

Berlin, James. 1988. Rhetoric and Ideology in the Writing Class. *College English* 50: 477–94.

———. 1994. The Subversions of the Portfolio. *New Directions in Portfolio Assessment,* ed. L. Black, D. Daiker, J. Sommers, and G. Stygall. Portsmouth, NH: Boynton/Cook.

Bizzell, Patricia. 1992. *Academic Discourse and Critical Consciousness.* Pittsburgh: Pittsburgh University Press.

Black, Laurel, Donald A. Daiker, Jeffrey Sommers, and Gail Stygall, ed. 1994. *New Directions in Portfolio Assessment: Reflective Practice, Critical Theory, and Large-Scale Scoring.* Portsmouth, NH: Boynton/Cook, Heinemann.

Black, Laurel, Edwina Helton and Jeffrey Sommers. 1994. Connecting Current Research on Authentic and Performance Assessment through Portfolios. *Assessing Writing* 1: 247–66.

Bleich, David. 1997. What Can Be Done About Grading. *Grading In the Post-Process Classroom: From Theory to Practice,* ed. L. Allison, L. Bryant and M. Hourigan. Portsmouth, NH: Boynton/Cook.

Bourdieu, Pierre and Loic J. D. Wacquant. 1992. *An Invitation to Reflexive Sociology.* Chicago: University of Chicago Press.

Boyd, Richard. 1998. The Origins and Evolution of Grading Student Writing: Pedagogical Imperatives and Cultural Anxieties. *The Theory and Practice of Grading Writing: Problems and Possibilities.* ed. F. Zak and C. Weaver. Albany: SUNY Press.

Brannon, Lil and Cy H. Knoblauch.1982. On Students' Right to Their Own Texts: A Model of Teacher Response. *College Composition and Communication* 33: 157–66.

Breland, Hunter. 1996. Computer-Assisted Writing Assessment: The Politics of Science versus Humanities. *Assessment of Writing: Politics, Policies, Practices,* ed. E. White, W. Lutz and S. Kamuskiri. NY: Modern Language Association.

Britton, James N., T. Burgess, N. Martin, A. McLeod, and H. Rosen. 1975. *The Development of Writing Abilities (11–18).* London: Macmillan Education Ltd.

Broad, Robert L. 1994. "Portfolio Scoring:" A Contradiction in Terms. *New Directions in Portfolio Assessment: Reflective Practice, Critical Theory, and Large-scale Scoring,* ed. L. Black, D. A. Daiker, J. Sommers, and G. Stygall. Portsmouth, NH: Boynton/Cook, Heinemann.

———. 1997. Reciprocal Authorities in Communal Writing Assessment: Constructing Textual Value Within a 'New Politics of Inquiry.' *Assessing Writing* 4: 133–68.

———. 2000. Pulling Your Hair Out: Crisis of Standardization in Communal Writing Assessment. *Research in the Teaching of English* 35: 213–60.

Brown, George and Gillian Yule.1983. *Discourse Analysis.* Cambridge: Cambridge University Press.

Bunch, Michael B. and Henry H. Scherich.1993. A Summary of the Reliability Studies in Holistic Writing Assessment. Presented at annual meeting of the American Educational Research Association. Atlanta, GA.

Callahan, Susan. 1997a. Tests Worth Taking?: Using Portfolios for Accountability in Kentucky. *Research in the Teaching of English* 31: 295–336.

———. 1997b. Kentucky's State-Mandated Writing Portfolios and Teacher Accountability. *Situating Portfolios: Four Perspectives,* ed. K. B. Yancey and I. Weiser. Logan: Utah State Press.

———. 1999. All Done with the Best of Intentions: One Kentucky High School After Six Years of State Portfolio Tests. *Assessing Writing* 6: 5–40.

Camp, Roberta and Denise S. Levine. 1991. Background and Variations in Sixth-Through Twelfth-Grade Classrooms. *Portfolios: Process and Product,* ed. P. Belanoff and M. Dickson. Portsmouth, NH: Boynton/Cook.

Camp Roberta. 1993. Changing the Model for the Direct Assessment of Writing. *Validating Holistic Scoring for Writing Assessment: Theoretical and Empirical Foundations,* ed. Michael M. Williamson and Brian Huot. Cresskill, NJ: Hampton.

———. 1996. Response: The Politics of Methodology. *Assessment of Writing: Politics, Policies, Practices,* ed. E. M. White, W. D. Lutz, and S. Kamuskiri. New York: Modern Language Association.

Carini, Patricia F. 1994. Dear Sister Bess: An Essay on Standards, Judgement and Writing. *Assessing Writing* 1: 29–65.

———. 2001. *Starting Strong: A Different Look at Children's Schools, and Standards.* New York: Teachers College Press.

Chappell, Virginia A. 1991. Teaching Like a Reader Instead of Reading Like a Teacher. *Balancing Acts: Essays on the Teaching of Writing in Honor of William F. Irmscher,* ed. V. A. Chappell, M. L. Buely-Meissner, and C. Anderson. Carbondale, IL: SIU Press.

Charney, Davida. 1984. The Validity of Using Holistic Scoring to Evaluate Writing: A Critical Overview. *Research in the Teaching of English* 18: 65–81.

Cherry, Roger and Paul Meyer. 1993. Reliability Issues in Holistic Assessment. *Validating Holistic Scoring for Writing Assessment: Theoretical and Empirical Foundations,* ed. M. M. Williamson and B. Huot. Cresskill, NJ: Hampton.

Cherry, Roger D. and Stephen P. Witte. 1998. Direct Assessments of Writing: Substance and Romance. *Assessing Writing* 5: 71–87.

Cherryholmes, Cleo H. 1988. *Power and Criticism: Poststructural Investigations in Education.* New York: Teachers College Press.

Combs, Warren and William L. Smith. 1980. The Effects of Overt and Covert Clues in Written Syntax. *Research in the Teaching of English* 14: 19–38.

Connors, Robert J. 1986. The Rhetoric of Mechanical Correctness. *Only Connect: Uniting Reading and Writing,* ed. T. Newkirk. Upper Montclair, NJ: Boynton/Cook.

Connors, Robert J. and Andrea A. Lunsford. 1993. Teachers' Rhetorical Comments on Student Papers. *College Composition and Communication* 44: 200–23.

Cooper, Charles R. 1977. Holistic Evaluation of Writing. *Evaluating Writing: Describing, Measuring and Judging.* ed. C. R. Cooper and L. Odell. Urbana, IL: NCTE 3–33.

Cooper, Peter. 1984. *The Assessment of Writing Ability: A Review of Research.* Princeton: Educational Testing Service: GREB No. 82–15R.

Cronbach, Lee J. 1971. Test Validation. *Educational Measurement,* 2nd ed., ed. R. L. Thorndike. Washington, DC: American Council on Education: 443–507.

———. 1988. Five Perspectives on Validity Argument. *Test Validity,* ed. H. Wainer. Hillside, NJ: Lawrence Erlbaum.

———. 1989. Construct Validity After Thirty Years. *Intelligence: Measurement Theory and Public Policy.* Urbana: University of Illinois Press:147–71.

Daiker, Donald A., Jeffrey Sommers, and Gail Stygall. 1996. The Pedagogical Implications of a College Placement Portfolio. *Assessment of Writing: Politics, Policies, Practices,* ed. E. M. White, W.

D. Lutz, and S. Kamuskiri. New York: Modern Language Association.

Davis, Barbara Gross, Michael Scriven, and Susan Thomas. 1987. *The Evaluation of Composition Instruction*, 2nd ed. New York: Teachers College Press.

Diederich, Paul B. 1974. *Measuring Growth in English*. Urbana: NCTE.

————. 1996. Turning Fords Into Lincolns: Reminiscences on Teaching and Assessing Writing. *Research in the Teaching of English* 30: 352–60.

Diederich, Paul B., John W. French and Sydell T. Carlton. 1961. *Factors in Judgments of Writing Quality*. Princeton: Educational Testing Service: RB No. 61–15. ED 002 172.

Durst, Russel. 1999. *Collision Course: Conflict Negotiation and Learning in College Composition*. Urbana: NCTE.

Durst, Russel, Marjorie Roemer, and Lucille Schultz. 1994. Portfolio Negotiations: Acts in Speech. *New Directions in Portfolio Assessment*, ed. L. Black, D. A. Daiker, J. Sommers, and G. Stygall, Portsmouth, NH: Boynton/Cook.

Elbow, Peter. 1973. *Writing Without Teachers*. New York: Oxford Press.

————. 1991. Foreword. *Portfolios: Process and Product*, ed. P. Belanoff and M. Dickson. Portsmouth, NH: Boynton/Cook.

————. 1993. Ranking, Evaluating, and Liking: Sorting Out Three Forms of Judgment. *College English* 55: 187–206.

————. 1994. Will the Virtues of Portfolios Blind Us to Their Potential Dangers? *New Directions in Portfolio Assessment: Reflective Practice, Critical Theory, and Large-scale Scoring*, ed. L. Black, D. A. Daiker, J. Sommers, and G. Stygall. Portsmouth, NH: Boynton/Cook.

————. 1996. Writing Assessment: Do it Better: Do it Less. *Assessment of Writing: Politics, Policies, Practices*, ed. E. M. White, W. D. Lutz, and S. Kamuskiri. New York: Modern Language Association.

————. 1998. Changing Grades While Working With Grades. *The Theory and Practice of Grading Writing: Problems and Possibilities*, ed. F. Zak and C. Weaver. Albany, NY: SUNY Press.

Elbow, Peter and Patricia Belanoff. 1991. State University of New York at Stony Brook Portfolio-based Evaluation Program. *Portfolios: Process and Product*, ed. P. Belanoff and M. Dickson. Portsmouth, NH: Boynton/Cook.

Emig, Janet A. 1971. *The Composing Processes of Twelfth Graders*. Urbana: NCTE.

Englehard, George Jr., Belita Gordon, and Stephen Gabrielson. 1992. The Influences of Mode of Discourse, Experiential Demand, and Gender on the Quality of Student Writing. *Research in the Teaching of English* 26: 315–36.

English Journal Focus: Assessing Assessment. 1994. *English Journal* 83: 37.

Faigley, Lester. 1989. Judging Writers, Judging Selves. *College Composition and Communication* 40: 395–412.

———. 1992. *Fragments of Rationality: Postmodernity and the Subject of Composition*. Pittsburgh: University of Pittsburgh Press.

Faigley, Lester, Roger Cherry, David A. Jolliffe, and Anna M. Skinner. 1985. *Assessing Writers' Knowledge and Processes of Composing*. Norwood: Ablex.

Feenburg, Andrew. 1991. *Critical Theory of Technology*. New York: Oxford Press.

Fife, Jane Mathison and Peggy O'Neill. 2001. Moving Beyond the Written Comment: Narrowing the Gap between Response Practice and Research. *College Composition and Communication* 53: 300–21.

Fish, Stanley. 1980. *Is There a Text in This Class?* Cambridge: Harvard University Press.

Fitzgerald, Kathryn R. 1996. From Disciplining to Discipline: A Foucauldian Examination of the Formation of English as a School Subject. *JAC: Journal of Composition Theory*: 436–53.

Foucault, Michel. 1977. *Discipline and Punish: The Birth of the Prison*. Trans. A. Sheridan. New York: Pantheon.

Freedman, Sarah W. 1984. The Registers of Student and Professional Expository Writing: Influences on Teachers' Responses. *New Directions in Composition Research*, ed. R. Beach and L. Bridwell. New York: Guilford.

Fuess, Claude. 1967. *The College Board: Its First Fifty Years*. New York: College Entrance Examination Board.

Gere, Anne Ruggles. 1980. Written Composition: Toward a Theory of Evaluation. *College English* 42: 44–58.

Gleason, Barbara. 2000. Evaluating Writing Programs in Real Time: The Politics of Remediation. *College Composition and Communication* 51: 560–89.

Godshalk, Fred I., Frances Swineford, and William E. Coffman. 1966. *The Measurement of Writing Ability.* Princeton: Educational Testing Service: CEEB RM No. 6.

Greenberg, Karen L., Harvey S. Wiener, and Richard A. Donovan, ed. 1986. *Writing Assessment: Issues and Strategies.* New York: Longman.

Guba, Egon G., ed. 1990. The Alternative Paradigm Dialog. *The Paradigm Dialog.* Newbury Park, CA: Sage.

Guba, Evon G., and Yvonna S. Lincoln. 1989. *Fourth Generation Evaluation.* Newbury Park, CA: Sage.

Guilford, J. P. 1946. New Standards for Test Evaluation. *Educational and Psychological Measurement* 6: 427–39.

Guion, Robert M. 1980. On Trinitarian Doctrines of Validity. *Professional Psychology* 11: 385–98.

Halliday, Michael A. K. 1978. *Language as Social Semiotic.* Baltimore: Edward Arnold.

Hake, Rosemary. 1986. How Do We Judge What They Write? *Writing Assessment: Issues and Strategies,* ed. K. Greenberg, H. Wiener and R. Donovan. New York: Longman.

Hamilton, Sharon. 1994. Portfolio Pedagogy: Is a Theoretical Construct Good Enough? *New Directions in Portfolio Assessment,* ed. L. Black, D. A. Daiker, J. Sommers, and G. Stygall. Portsmouth, NH: Boynton/Cook.

Hanson, F. Allen. 1993. *Testing Testing: the Social Consequences of an Examined Life.* Berkeley: California University Press.

Harris, Joseph. 1996. Personal correspondence.

Haswell, Richard. 1998. Multiple Inquiry in the Validation of Writing Tests. *Assessing Writing* 5: 89–109.

———, ed. 2001. *Beyond Outcomes: Assessment and Instruction Within a University Writing Program.* Westport, CT: Ablex.

Haswell, Richard and Susan McCleod. 1997. WAC Assessment and Internal Audiences: A Dialogue. *Assessing Writing Across the Curriculum: Diverse Approaches and Practices.* Greenwich, CT: Ablex.

Haswell, Richard, and Susan Wyche-Smith. 1994. Adventuring into Writing Assessment. *College Composition and Communications* 45: 220–236.

———. 1995. A Two-Tiered Rating Procedure for Placement Essays. *Assessment in Practice: Putting Principles to Work on College Campuses,* ed. T. Banta. San Francisco: Jossey-Bass.

Hawisher, Gail. 1989. Research and Recommendations for Computers and Composition. *Critical Perspectives on Computers and Computer Instruction,* ed. Gail Hawisher and Cynthia Selfe. New York: Teachers College Press.

Hayes, Mary F., and Donald A. Daiker. 1984. Using Protocol Analysis in Evaluating Responses to Student Writing. *Freshman English News* 13: 1–10.

Hester, Vicki, Brian Huot, Michael Neal, and Peggy O'Neill. 2000. Reporting on the Results and Implications of a Six-Year Pilot Program Using Portfolios to Place Students in First-Year College Composition. Presented at American Educational Association annual conference. New Orleans.

Hilgers, Thomas H. 1984. Toward a Taxonomy of Beginning Writers' Evaluative Statements on Written Compositions. *Written Communication* 1: 365–84.

———. 1986. How Children Change as Critical Evaluators of Writing: Four Three-Year Case Studies. *Research in the Teaching of English* 20: 36–55.

Hillocks, George Jr. 1995. *Teaching Writing as Reflective Practice.* New York: Teachers College Press.

Himley, Margaret. 1989. A Reflective Conversation: Tempos of Meaning. *Encountering Student Texts,* ed. B. Lawson, S. Sterr Ryan, and R. W. Winterowd. Urbana: NCTE.

Hoetker, James. 1982. Essay Examination Topics and Students' Writing. *College Composition and Communication* 33: 377–92.

Hopkins, Thomas L. 1921. The Marking System of the College Entrance Examination Board. *Harvard Monographs in Education* Series 1 No. 2. Cambridge, MA.

Huot, Brian. 1990a. The Literature of Direct Writing Assessment: Major Concerns and Prevailing Trends. *Review of Educational Research* 60: 237–64.

————. 1990b. Reliability, Validity, and Holistic Scoring: What We Know and What We Need to Know. *College Composition and Communication* 41: 201–213.

————. 1993. The Influence of Holistic Scoring Procedures on Reading and Rating Student Essays. *Validating Holistic Scoring for Writing Assessment: Theoretical and Empirical Foundations,* ed. M. M. Williamson and B. Huot. Cresskill, NJ: Hampton.

————. 1994a. A Survey of College and University Placement Practices. *WPA: Writing Program Administration* 17: 49–67.

————. 1994b. Beyond the Classroom: Using Portfolios to Assess Writing. *New Directions in Portfolio Assessment,* ed. L. Black, D. A. Daiker, J. Sommers, and G. Stygall. Portsmouth, NH: Boynton/Cook.

————. 1994c. An Introduction to Assessing Writing. *Assessing Writing* 1: 1–9.

————. 1996. Toward a New Theory of Writing Assessment. *College Composition and Communication* 47: 549–66.

Huot, Brian and Michael M. Williamson. 1997. Rethinking Portfolios for Evaluating Writing: Issues of Assessment and Power. *Situating Portfolios: Four Perspectives,* ed. K. B. Yancey and I. Weiser. Logan: Utah State University Press.

Iser, Wolfgang. 1978. *The Act of Reading: A Theory of Aesthetic Response.* Baltimore: Johns Hopkins University Press.

Johanek, Cindy. 2000. *Composing Research: A Contextualist Paradigm for Rhetoric and Composition.* Logan: Utah State University Press.

Johnston, Peter. 1989. Constructive Evaluation and the Improvement of Teaching and Learning. *Teachers College Record* 90: 509–28.

Judine, Sister M. 1965. *A Guide for Evaluating Student Compositions.* Urbana: NCTE.

Klein, Julie Thompson. 1990. *Interdisciplinarity: History, Theory, and Practice.* Detroit: Wayne State University Press.

Koretz, Daniel. 1993. The Evaluation of the Vermont Portfolio Program: Interpretations of Initial Findings. Annual Meeting of the National Council of Measurement in Education. Atlanta.

Labov, William, ed. 1980. *Locating Language in Time and Space.* New York: Academic Press.

Larson, Richard L. 1996. Portfolios in the Assessment of Writing: A Political Perspective. *Assessment of Writing: Politics Policies and Practices*, ed. E. White, W. Lutz, and S. Kamuskiri. New York: Modern Language Association.

———. 2000. Revision as Self-Assessment. *Self-Assessment and Development in Writing*, ed. Smith, J. B. and K. B. Yancey. Cresskill, NJ: Hampton.

Lawson, Bruce, Susan Sterr Ryan, and W. Ross Winterowd, ed. 1989. *Encountering Student Texts: Interpretive Issues in Reading Student Writing*. Urbana: NCTE.

Lehmann, Nicholas. 1999. *The Big Test: The Secret History of the American Meritocracy*. New York: Farrar, Straus and Giroux.

Levinson, Stephen C. 1983. *Pragmatics*. New York: Cambridge University Press.

Lloyd–Jones, Richard. 1977. Primary Trait Scoring. *Evaluating Writing: Describing, Measuring and Judging*, ed. C. R. Cooper and L. Odell. Urbana: NCTE.

Lowe, Teresa J. and Brian Huot. 1997. Using KIRIS Writing Portfolios to Place Students in First–Year Composition at the University of Louisville. *Kentucky English Bulletin* 46: 46–64.

Lunsford, Andrea A. 1986. The Past and Future of Writing Assessment. *Writing Assessment: Issues and Strategies*, ed. K. L. Greenberg, H. S. Wiener, and R. A. Donovan. New York: Longman.

Madhaus, George F. 1993. A National Testing System: Manna From Above? An Historical/Technological Perspective. *Educational Assessment* 1: 9–28.

Marting, Janet. 1991. Writers on Writing: Assessment Strategies for Student Essays. *Teaching English in the Two-Year College* 18: 128–32.

Messick, Samuel. 1989a. Meaning and Values in Test Validation: The Science and Ethics of Assessment. *Educational Researcher* 18: 5–11.

———. 1989b. Validity. *Educational Measurement Third Edition*, ed. R. Linn. Washington, DC: American Council on Education and National Council on Measurement in Education.

Miller, Richard. 1994. Composing English Studies: Toward a Social History of the Discipline. *College Composition and Communication* 45: 164–79.

Miller, Susan. 1982. How Writers Evaluate Their Own Writing. *College Composition and Communication* 33: 176–83.

Mills-Court, Karen, and Minda Rae Amiran. 1991. Metacognition and the Use of Portfolios. *Portfolios: Process and Product,* ed. P. Belanoff and M. Dickson. Portsmouth, NH: Boynton/Cook.

Moss, Pamela A. 1992. Shifting Conceptions of Validity in Educational Measurement: Implications for Performative Assessment. *Review of Educational Research* 62: 229–258.

———. 1994a. Can There Be Validity Without Reliability? *Educational Researcher* 23: 5–12.

———. 1994b. Validity in High Stakes Writing Assessment: Problems and Possibilities. *Assessing Writing* 1: 109–28.

———. 1996. Enlarging the Dialogue in Educational Measurement: Voices from Interpretive Research Traditions. *Educational Researcher* 25.1: 20–28.

———. 1998. Response: Testing the Test of the Test. *Assessing Writing* 5: 111–22.

Moss, Pamela A. and Aaron Schutz. 2001. Educational Standards, Assessment and the Search for Consensus. *American Educational Research Journal* 38: 37–70.

Murphy, Sandra. 1994. Portfolios and Curriculum Reform: Patterns in Practice. *Assessing Writing* 1: 175–206.

———. 1997. Teachers and Students: Reclaiming Assessment Via Portfolios. *Situating Portfolios: Four Perspectives,* ed. K. B. Yancey and I. Weiser. Logan: Utah State University Press.

———. 2000. A Sociocultural Perspective on Teacher Response: Is There a Student in the Room? *Assessing Writing* 7: 79–90.

Murphy, Sandra, and Barbara Grant. 1996. Portfolio Approaches to Assessment: Breakthrough or More of the Same? *Assessment of Writing: Politics, Policies, Practices,* ed. E. M. White, W. D. Lutz, and S. Kamuskiri. New York: Modern Language Association.

Murphy, Sandra, and Leo Ruth. 1993. The Field Testing of Writing Prompts Reconsidered. *Validating Holistic Scoring for Writing Assessment: Theoretical and Empirical Foundations,* ed. M. Williamson and B. Huot. Cresskill, NJ: Hampton.

Myers, Miles. 1980. *A Procedure for Writing Assessment and Holistic Scoring.* Urbana: NCTE.

Nelson, Jeannie. 1995. Reading Classrooms as Text: Exploring Student Writers' Interpretive Practices. *College Composition and Communication* 46: 411–29.

North, Stephen M. 1987. *The Making of Knowledge in Composition: Portrait of an Emerging Field.* Upper Montclair, NJ: Boynton-Cook.

Nystrand, Martin, Alan S. Cohen, and Nora M. Dowling. 1993. Addressing Reliability Problems in the Portfolio Assessment of College Writing. *Educational Assessment* 1: 53–70.

Olson, Gary A. 1999. Toward a Post–Process Composition: Abandoning the Rhetoric of Assertion. *Post-Process Theory: Beyond the Writing Process Paradigm,* ed. Thomas Kent. Carbondale, IL: SIU Press.

O'Neill, Peggy. 1998. Writing Assessment and the Disciplinarity of Composition. Ph.D. dissertation, University of Louisville.

Palmer, Orville. 1960. Sixty Years of English Testing. *College Board Review* 42: 8–14.

Papert, Seymour. 1987. Computer Criticism Versus Technocentric Thinking. *Educational Researcher* 16: 22–30.

Papoulis, Irene. 1998. Gender and Grading: 'Immanence' as a Path to 'Transcendence?' *The Theory and Practice of Grading Writing: Problems and Possibilities,* ed. F. Zak and C. Weaver. Albany, NY: SUNY Press.

Phelps, Louise Wetherbee. 1989. Images of Student Writing: The Deep Structure of Teacher Response. *Writing and Response: Theory, Practice and Research,* ed. Chris M. Anson. Urbana: NCTE.

———. 1998. Surprised by Response: Student, Teacher, Editor, Reviewer. *JAC: A Journal of Composition Theory* 18: 247–73.

———. 2000. Cyrano's Nose: Variations on the Theme of Response. *Assessing Writing* 7: 91–110.

Pula, Judith J., and Brian Huot. 1993. A Model of Background Influences on Holistic Raters. *Validating Holistic Scoring for Writing Assessment: Theoretical and Empirical Foundations,* ed. M. M. Williamson and B. Huot. Cresskill, NJ: Hampton.

Purves, Alan C. 1992. Reflections on Research and Assessment in Written Composition. *Research in the Teaching of English* 26: 108–22.

———. 1995. Apologia Not Accepted. *College Composition and Communication* 46: 549–50.

————. 1996. Personal communication, December.

Qualley, Donna. 2002. Learning to Evaluate and Grade Student Writing. *Preparing College Teachers of Writing: Histories, Theories, Programs, Practices,* ed. B. Pytlik and S. Liggett. New York: Oxford University Press.

Resnick, Lauren, and David Resnick. 1982. Assessing the Thinking Curriculum: New Tools for Educational Reform. *Changing Assessments: Alternative Views of Aptitude Achievement and Instruction,* ed. B. R. Gifford and M. C. O'Connor. Boston: Flower.

Rigsby, Leo. 1987. Changes in Student Writing and Their Significance. Conference on College Composition and Communication annual convention. Atlanta.

Royer, Daniel J., and Roger Gilles. 1998. Directed Self–Placement: An Attitude of Orientation. *College Composition and Communication* 50: 54–70.

Ruth, Leo and Sandra Murphy. 1988. *Designing Writing Tasks for the Assessment of Writing.* Norwood, NJ: Ablex.

Scharton, Maurice. 1996. The Politics of Validity. *Assessment of Writing: Politics, Policies, Practices,* ed. E. White, W. Lutz and S. Kamuskiri. New York: Modern Language Association.

Schendel, Ellen and Peggy O'Neill. 1999. Exploring the Theories and Consequences of Self–Assessment through Ethical Inquiry. *Assessing Writing* 6: 199–227.

Schön, Donald A. 1983. *The Reflective Practitioner: How Professionals Think in Action.* New York: Basic Books.

Shepard, Lorrie A. 1993. Evaluating Test Validity. *Review of Research in Education.* 19: 405–450.

Shiffman, Betty Garrison. 1997. Grading Student Writing: The Dilemma from a Feminist Perspective. *Grading In the Post-Process Classroom: From Theory to Practice,* ed. L. Allison, L. Bryant and M. Hourigan. Portsmouth, NH: Boynton/Cook.

Shumacher, Gary and Jane Gradwohl Nash. 1991. Conceptualizing and Measuring Knowledge Change Due to Writing. *Research in the Teaching of Writing* 25: 67–96.

Smith, Barbara Hernstein. 1988. *Contingencies of Value: Alternative Perspectives for Critical Theory.* Cambridge, MA: Harvard University Press.

Smith, Frank. 1982. *Understanding Reading*, 3rd ed. New York: Holt.

Smith, Jane Bowman, and Kathleen Blake Yancey. 2000. *Self-Assessment and Development in Writing*. Cresskill, NJ: Hampton.

Smith, William L. 1993. Assessing the Reliability and Adequacy of Using Holistic Scoring of Essays as a College Composition Placement Program Technique. *Validating Holistic Scoring for Writing Assessment: Theoretical and Empirical Foundations*, ed. M. M. Williamson and B. Huot. Cresskill, NJ: Hampton.

Sommers, Nancy. 1982. Responding to Student Writing. *College Composition and Communication* 33: 148–56.

Spaulding, Elizabeth and Gail Cummins. 1998. It Was the Best of Times, It Was a Waste of Time: University of Kentucky Students' View of Writing Under KERA. *Assessing Writing* 5: 167–200.

Speck, Bruce W., and Tommy R. Jones. 1998. Direction in the Grading of Writing: What the Literature on the Grading of Writing Does and Doesn't Tell Us. *The Theory and Practice of Grading Writing: Problems and Possibilities*, ed. F. Zak and C. Weaver. Albany, NY: SUNY Press.

Sperling, Melanie. 1994. Constructing the Perspective of Teacher-as-Reader: A Framework for Studying Response to Student Writing. *Research in the Teaching of English* 28: 175–207.

Sperling, Melanie, and Sarah W. Freedman. 1987. A Good Girl Writes Like a Good Girl: Written Response and Clues to the Teaching/Learning Process. *Written Communication* 4: 343–69.

Starch, Daniel, and Edward C. Elliott. 1912. Reliability of the Grading of High-School Work in English. *School Review* 20: 442–57.

Stock, Patricia L. and Jay L. Robinson. 1987. Taking on Testing: Teachers as Tester-Researchers. *English Education* 19: 93–121.

Straub, Richard. 1996. The Concept of Control in Teacher Response: Defining the Varieties of Directive and Facilitative Commentary. *College Composition and Communication* 47: 223–51.

———. 1997. Students' Reactions to Teachers' Comments: An Exploratory Study. *Research in the Teaching of English* 31: 91–120.

———. 2000. The Student, the Test and the Classroom Context: A Case Study of Teacher Response. *Assessing Writing* 7: 23–56.

Straub, Richard, and Ronald F. Lunsford. 1995. *Twelve Readers Reading: Responding to College Student Writing.* Cresskill, NJ: Hampton.

Sulieman, Susan R. 1980. Introduction: Varieties of Audience-Oriented Criticism. *The Reader in the Text,* ed. S. R. Sulieman and I. Crosman. Princeton: Princeton University Press.

Sunstein, Bonnie. 1996. Assessing Assessment and Reflecting on Reflection: The Mirror and the Scoreboard. Presented at NCTE Conference on Learning and Literacies. Albuquerque.

Sunstein, Bonnie, and Jonathan Lovell, ed. 2000. *The Portfolio Standard: How Students Can Show Us What They Know and How They Know It.* Portsmouth, NH: Heinemann.

Thelin, William. 1994. The Connection Between Response Styles and Portfolio Assessment: Three Case Studies of Student Revision. *New Directions in Portfolio Assessment,* ed. L. Black, D. Daiker, J. Sommers, and G. Stygall. Portsmouth, NH: Boynton/Cook.

Tierney, Robert J. and P. David Pearson. 1983. Toward a Composing Model of Reading. *Language Arts* 60: 568–80.

Tobin, Lad. 1991. Reading Students, Reading Ourselves: Revising The Teacher's Role in the Writing Class. *College English* 53: 333–48.

Trachsel, Mary. 1992. *Institutionalizing Literacy: The Historical Role of College Entrance Examinations in English.* Carbondale, IL: SIU Press.

Valentine, John A. 1987. *The College Board and the School Curriculum: A History of the College Board's Influence on the Substance and Standards of American Education 1900–1980.* New York: College Entrance Examination Board.

Veal, Ramon L. and Sally A. Hudson. 1983. Direct and Indirect Measures for the Large-Scale Evaluation of Writing. *Research in the Teaching of English* 17: 285–96.

White, Edward M. 1990. Language and Reality in Writing Assessment. *College Composition and Communication* 40: 187–200.

———. 1993. Holistic Scoring: Past Triumphs and Future Challenges. *Validating Holistic Scoring for Writing Assessment: Theoretical and Empirical Foundations,* ed. M. M. Williamson and B. Huot. Cresskill, NJ: Hampton.

————. 1994a. *Teaching and Assessing Writing, 2nd ed.* San Francisco: Jossey-Bass.

————. 1994b. Issues and Problems in Writing Assessment. *Assessing Writing* 1: 11–27.

————. 1995a. Apologia for the Timed Impromptu Essay Test. *College Composition and Communication* 46: 30–45.

————. 1995b. Response To Alan Purves. *College Composition and Communication* 46: 550–51.

White, Edward M., William D. Lutz, and Sandra Kamuskiri, ed. 1996. *Assessment of Writing: Politics, Policies, Practices.* New York: Modern Language Association.

Wiggins, Grant. 1993. *Assessing Student Performance.* San Francisco: Jossey Bass.

Williams, Joseph. 1981. The Phenomenology of Error. *College Composition and Communication* 32: 152–68.

Williamson, Michael M. 1993. An Introduction to Holistic Scoring: The Social, Historical, and Theoretical Context for Writing Assessment. *Validating Holistic Scoring for Writing Assessment: Theoretical and Empirical Foundations,* ed. M. M. Williamson and B. Huot. Cresskill, NJ: Hampton.

————. 1994. The Worship of Efficiency: Untangling Theoretical and Practical Considerations in Writing Assessment. *Assessing Writing* 1: 147–74.

Williamson, Michael M., and Brian Huot, ed. 1993. *Validating Holistic Scoring for Writing Assessment: Theoretical and Empirical Foundations.* Cresskill, NJ: Hampton.

Winner, Langdon. 1986. *The Whale and the Reactor: A Search for Limits in an Age of High Technology.* Chicago: Chicago University Press.

Witte, Stephen P., Mary Trachsel, and Keith Walters. 1986. Literacy and the Direct Assessment of Writing: A Diachronic Approach. *Writing Assessment: Issues and Strategies,* ed. Karen L. Greenberg, Harvey S. Wiener, and Richard A. Donovan. New York: Longman.

Yancey, Kathleen Blake. 1992. *Portfolios in the Writing Classroom: An Introduction,* ed. Kathleen Blake Yancey. Urbana, IL: NCTE.

————. 1998. *Reflection in the Writing Classroom.* Logan: Utah State University Press.

————. 1999. Looking Back as We Look Forward: Historicizing Writing Assessment. *College Composition and Communication* 50: 483–503.

Yancey, Kathleen Blake, and Irwin Weiser, ed. 1997. *Situating Portfolios: Four Perspectives.* Logan: Utah State University Press.

Zak, Frances, and Christopher C. Weaver. 1998. *The Theory and Practice of Grading Writing: Problems and Possibilities.* Albany, NY: SUNY Press.

Zebroski, James T. 1989. A Hero in the Classroom. *Encountering Student Texts: Interpretive Issues in Reading Student Writing,* ed. B. Lawson, S. Sterr Ryan, and W. R. Winterowd. Urbana: NCTE.

————. 1994. *Thinking Through Theory: Vygotskian Perspectives on the Teaching of Writing.* Portsmouth, NH: Boynton/Cook.

————. 1998. Toward a Theory of Theory for Composition Studies. *Under Construction: Working at the Intersections of Composition Theory, Research, and Practice,* ed. C. Farris and C. Anson. Logan: Utah State University Press.

INDEX

BRIAN HUOT is Professor of English and Director of Composition at the University of Louisville. His published work has appeared in *College Composition and Communication*, *College English*, *WPA: Writing Program Administration* and other journals and collections devoted to the teaching and assessing of writing. He is co-founder and was co-editor of *Assessing Writing* from 1994–2000; more recently he co-founded and continues to co-edit *The Journal of Writing Assessment*.